Show
the Value
of What
You Do

Show the Value of What You Do

MEASURING AND ACHIEVING SUCCESS IN ANY ENDEAVOR

Patricia Pulliam Phillips
CEO of ROI Institute

Jack J. Phillips
Chair of ROI Institute

BK

Berrett–Koehler Publishers, Inc.

Berrett-Koehler Publishers, Inc.
1333 Broadway, Suite 1000
Oakland, CA 94612-1921
Tel: (510) 817-2277
Fax: (510) 817-2278
www.bkconnection.com

ORDERING INFORMATION

Quantity sales. Special discounts are available on quantity purchases by corporations, associations, and others. For details, contact the "Special Sales Department" at the Berrett-Koehler address above.

Individual sales. Berrett-Koehler publications are available through most bookstores. They can also be ordered directly from Berrett-Koehler: Tel: (800) 929-2929; Fax: (802) 864-7626; www.bkconnection.com.

Orders for college textbook / course adoption use. Please contact Berrett-Koehler: Tel: (800) 929-2929; Fax: (802) 864-7626.

Distributed to the U.S. trade and internationally by Penguin Random House Publisher Services.

Berrett-Koehler and the BK logo are registered trademarks of Berrett-Koehler Publishers, Inc.

Printed in Canada

Berrett-Koehler books are printed on long-lasting acid-free paper. When it is available, we choose paper that has been manufactured by environmentally responsible processes. These may include using trees grown in sustainable forests, incorporating recycled paper, minimizing chlorine in bleaching, or recycling the energy produced at the paper mill.

Library of Congress Cataloging-in-Publication Data
Names: Phillips, Patricia Pulliam, author. | Phillips, Jack J., 1945- author.
Title: Show the value of what you do : measuring and achieving success in any
    endeavor / Patricia Pulliam Phillips and Jack J. Phillips.
Description: First edition. | Oakland, CA : Berrett-Koehler Publishers, [2022] |
    Includes bibliographical references and index.
Identifiers: LCCN 2022009310 (print) | LCCN 2022009311 (ebook) |
    ISBN 9781523002276 (paperback ; alk. paper) | ISBN 9781523002283 (pdf) |
    ISBN 9781523002290 (epub) | ISBN 9781523002306
Subjects: LCSH: Organizational effectiveness—Measurement. | Performance—
    Measurement. | Value.
Classification: LCC HD58.9 .P5185 2022 (print) | LCC HD58.9 (ebook) |
    DDC 658—dc23/eng/20220324
LC record available at https://lccn.loc.gov/2022009310
LC ebook record available at https://lccn.loc.gov/2022009311

First Edition
27 26 25 24 23 22   10 9 8 7 6 5 4 3 2 1

Book producer: Westchester Publishing Services
Cover designer: Matt Avery

THIS BOOK IS DEDICATED

to our family

who always support us in all our endeavors,

to our amazing team at ROI Institute

who provide excellent service to our customers, and

to our loyal customer base

who inspire us to do our very best.

Contents

Delivering Success

Sometimes the value of the work, the projects you undertake, or the initiatives you tackle are unclear. In this era of evidence-based inquiry, value needs to be credible, accurate, and compelling. ROI Institute has been addressing this issue with a process called the ROI Methodology for the past three decades.

The Show the Value Process is a simplified version of the Return on Investment (ROI) Methodology. This book describes six easy steps to measure and improve the success of any project, program, initiative, or work that you do. It will help you avoid disappointing results by designing for and delivering the desired outcome. It is logical, credible, and easy to use.

We developed the ROI Methodology in the 1970s and refined it in the 1980s when the first book describing the process was published. It was implemented globally in the 1990s and since then has become one of the most used evaluation systems in the world, as it is used routinely in more than 6,000 organizations in 70 countries. Our team has written over 75 books to support the ROI Methodology, including case study contributions from users of the process. Over the years, we have refined the process to make it more successful, with users approving the standards guiding it. In essence, the ROI Methodology is a credible, CEO-friendly, and user-centered process. With our team, we have trained more than 50,000 managers and professionals in the ROI Methodology. And, we have used the methodology in thousands of studies to measure the impact and ROI of projects, programs, and initiatives.

But let's face it, data and data analysis frighten people, ROI frightens people, and a 500-page book *really* frightens people! It doesn't have to be this way. Our process is relatively simple. It provides a way of thinking about the work that you do, the projects that you pursue, and the definition you place on success. It helps you think about how to drive success and measure that success at different levels and from different perspectives. It also helps you decide if the project is worth implementing. The Show the Value Process described in this book will make a difference in your work and the projects you undertake.

THREE GOALS FOR THIS BOOK

The **first goal** is to help individuals and teams achieve and measure the success of any new project, program, or initiative. For example, Reverend Doug Stewart shows the value of having a chaplain in the intensive care unit; Katie Westwood shows the value of a tuition refund program for a Fortune 50 company; Major Chip Huth, a police SWAT team leader, shows the value of a leadership program designed to reduce complaints about excessive force; Paula Patel shows the value of working at home; Anna Chen shows the value of a "Leader in Me" program to make seventh and eighth grade students more successful; and, finally, Sarah Robertson needed to show the value of counseling at a food bank. These are just six of the dozens of stories presented in the book, illustrating the vast applications of this process.

A review of applications that use this process reveals that it works in any situation and any work, job, or project for individuals and organizations. In addition to being effective in businesses, it is effective in governments, nongovernmental organizations (NGOs), nonprofits, school systems, charities, foundations, and associations. It works in different countries with all types of initiatives, from very soft programs, such as coaching, to hard programs, such as implementing a new IT system.

A **second goal** is to shift the thinking about projects and work from merely completed activities to investments that deliver impact. There are many misconceptions about what success means, and success itself varies. We mistakenly assume that you achieve success just by doing something. While activity is necessary, success comes when the activity's impact or consequence is evident. For example, historically, managers would applaud employee performance based on their workload, the length of the task completion list, and the fact that employees are visible at the office. Today, flexible work arrangements require a new way of measuring employee success on the job. No longer is performance measured by what people do and where they do it. Today, performance is measured by outcomes and the quality of those outcomes. Mere activity without a purposeful consequence means little—it is just being busy.

A **third goal** is to help you use project results to make improvements, increase support, and perhaps secure more funding in the future. The work is not over upon delivery of a successful project. It is vital to leverage a project's success for maximum results, and one way to do this is to always improve the project the next time around.

This book should become an indispensable guide for individuals and organizations who want to do work that matters and to demonstrate that it does. We see this book as a critical resource for professional groups, associations, and organizations to help their employees, associates, and members achieve success with what they do.

THE AUDIENCES AND USES

This book is a step-by-step guide to show the value of your work. Although appropriate for almost anyone, five specific audiences will especially find this book to be helpful:

1. Individual contributors will find this book valuable in helping them make progress in an organization. Individual contributors are those in professional, technical, creative, or support roles who want to make a difference in what they do.

2. Independent contractors and independent consultants (external or internal) will find this book valuable for their growth and success. This audience includes consultants, coaches, counselors, mentors, and advisors who need to demonstrate their contribution to the organization or community.

3. Experienced professionals will also find this book to be helpful to boost a blocked career. Although you may have a wealth of experience, some professionals may be stuck in a job assignment and not changing, advancing, or learning. This book will show you how to broaden your horizons as you demonstrate the value of what you do, attract the attention of others, and gain the recognition and success you need.

4. Team leaders, managers, and project managers will find this book to be a valuable resource to show the contribution of the work you are performing or the team's work. In most cases, it is the team's work that reflects on the team leader's performance. This book describes how to capture value from team accomplishments and contributions. It is also practical for small and medium-size organizations where limited time and resources may make it difficult to assess the success of a project or initiative.

5. Finally, career development professionals will find this book valuable as you help individuals and teams achieve success, improve performance, and advance in an organization.

IMPACT

When faced with an initiative to show the value of work, a new project for a particular group or client, or a new program involving others, most individuals do not have a systematic approach to achieving success, measuring that success, or reporting that success. Table 1 shows the traditional approach to this dilemma and the Show the Value approach, which this book presents.

The profile outlined in the traditional approach is a good example of what individuals are doing. Following it, however, leads

Table 1. Delivering and Measuring Success

Traditional Approach	Show the Value Approach
1. Start doing things with no end goal.	1. Start with the end in mind.
2. Have no system or process to achieve success.	2. Follow six steps to achieve success.
3. Rarely achieve the end goal.	3. Design for and achieve desired goals.
4. Focus on activities instead of results.	4. Deliver results on activities including impact and ROI.

to a project or initiative that suffers, contributing little value. Alternatively, following the Show the Value approach, as described in this book, essentially guarantees success for the project, making life easier and creating a situation that is easily repeatable with other projects.

Show the Value of What You Do will have three significant outcomes:

1. **It will change your approach.** As mentioned above, the book will change your mindset on defining and achieving success and improving future results. You will never view success again using the traditional paradigm.
2. **Your projects will be more successful.** The most significant outcome will be achieving the success of your personal or professional projects or initiatives. Just measuring the value helps you to achieve more value and will be realized with this process.
3. **It will help you, your work, and your organization.** As you measure success, report outcomes, and make improvements, you will find the results of these projects will be beneficial to you, your organization, and your community.

This book will help ensure that you keep your work relevant, your career on track, and your organization or community healthy. It will help ensure you allocate resources to the areas that offer the most significant value.

CUSTOMIZED WEBSITE

A portion of ROI Institute's website is dedicated to support this book as you pursue the journey of measuring the success of a project. Access this website at roiinstitute.net/show-the-value. The website will support you as you apply what you learn in the book. The website is designed to achieve four important goals:

1. **Inspiration.** The website will contain additional comments and praise about the book, adding to those on the back cover. It will provide more detail on many stories in the book so you can see the complete story. The website will also contain additional case studies showing how this process has been used by others beyond those presented in the book.

2. **Support.** The website will provide you an opportunity to request a discussion with one of ROI Institute's team members. You can obtain help with your project if you need it. Assessments, tips, and friendly advice are provided for each chapter.

3. **Tools.** Additional materials to enable the use of the process presented in this book will be available, including job aides, guides, templates, and in some cases, actual case studies highlighting how particular issues can be addressed.

4. **Learning Opportunities.** Additional learning opportunities supporting this book will be described on the website and include:

   - A one-day workshop
   - A train-the-trainer workshop
   - An ROI Certification process
   - Coaching to support you with the application of the process

THE FLOW OF THE BOOK

Chapter 1, "Show the Value Process," explores how to demonstrate value and describes the complete Show the Value Process model and why it is needed. It sets the stage and provides a preview of the entire book.

Chapter 2, "Why? Start with Impact," explains the first step of the process. This chapter describes the importance of connecting your project with a business measure, that is, an impact measure. Essentially, you begin with the end in mind.

Chapter 3 "How? Select the Right Solution," covers taking steps to ensure that your idea for the solution is the right one. Or, if it is a problem you are facing, you have to analyze the cause of the problem, which leads to the solution. Either way, you take steps to ensure you start on the right path.

Chapter 4, "What? Expect Success with Objectives," emphasizes the importance of measuring the impact to define the success needed for the project. Then, objectives are set for different levels of outcomes, from reaction to learning, application, impact, and even ROI. These objectives are critical to designing for the success that you need.

Chapter 5, "How Much? Collect Data along the Way," shows how data will need to be collected, whether formally or informally, along the chain of value, from reaction all the way to impact. Data collection doesn't have to be complicated, and the different ways to do this are fully explored.

Chapter 6, "What's It Worth? Analyze the Data," details in a nonthreatening way how the data analysis is pursued, with a focus on making it credible throughout the process. The actual ROI is calculated, if needed.

Chapter 7, "So What? Leverage the Results," begins with presenting the results to the right audiences. We'll share how to leverage the results to make the project better and influence others to earn more respect and improve the situation for all stakeholders.

Finally, the conclusion, "Making It Work," is a call to action. You will find advice and useful tips to get started with the Show the Value Process. All this knowledge without action would be a waste.

Overall, we think you will find this book to be a valuable reference and companion. Its content includes stories describing how others have used the Show the Value Process and found success. We hope you will find it insightful, challenging, engaging, and rewarding as you attempt to Show the Value of your work, projects, and initiatives.

CHAPTER I

Show the Value Process

MYTH: It is extremely difficult to show the value of the work that you do.

REALITY: Showing the value of what you do is a logical, easy process.

Reverend Bruce Fenner, director of endorsement for The United Methodist Church (UMC), knew there was a growing need for chaplains to demonstrate the value of their work. He recognized mere trust in spiritual care was no longer evidence enough; more tangible data was required if chaplaincy was to continue receiving funding, particularly in health care, the military, and even corporate settings. So, he and The UMC General Board of Higher Education and Ministry decided to host a workshop of approximately 57 chaplains. We facilitated that workshop. There we met Reverend Doug Stewart, chief chaplain at Memorial Hospital in Belleville, Illinois. Doug was one of many participants recognizing the need to show how chaplaincy contributes to organizational outcomes. He immediately saw the pertinence of our process to his work. He knew that failure to connect the work of chaplaincy to organizational outcomes would put funding for chaplaincy intervention at risk.

Many people argue that chaplaincy is a worthy investment that transcends the need for hardline accountability. It's hard not to trust a chaplain, right? But our work with Doug and others in

similar situations tells a different story. Creating and demonstrating value for investments in projects, processes, and inter-
ventions has never been more important. Options for spending
on activities to improve organizational, societal, and environmental outcomes are wide open. Many options cost little and are
often selected because of the minimal financial commitment.
And while proponents of investing in more expensive solutions
believe "you get what you pay for," the important question is "Do
you really?" This chapter introduces the Show the Value Process
that helps Doug and thousands of others show the value of
their work.

THE SEARCH FOR SUCCESS MEASURES

Why do you do the work you do? The specific work—the project
you are working on now, in fact. How will you demonstrate the
value of that project, or the system you are installing, or the new
procedure you are implementing? Defining success in clear
terms is the first step to demonstrate the value of what you do.
But as they say, the first step is always the hardest. Too often we
try to select one or two measures that, in the end, fail to communicate real value. That is because the measures may represent
only one viewpoint or type of data. Here are some categories of
measures that reflect different perspectives of value.

Happiness, commitment, and motivation. Reaction from
the project team defines success. The perception of a project by
team members is a vital measure of success. Are they happy with
it? Are they committed to making it work? If answers to these
questions are negative, there is a likelihood the project won't get
off dead center. And while important, these measures are not
enough.

Learning and capability. Sometimes the acquisition of
knowledge, skills, and credentials, as part of a project, may indicate success. Without a doubt, if you learn new knowledge and
develop new skills to make a project work, there is opportunity

to contribute additional value to the organization. But these measures of success are not enough. Knowledge is important, but it is only powerful when it is used.

Habits, behaviors, and actions. Routine and systematic actions are indicators of success. People are on the move; things are happening. So what? Action or behavior change without a purpose is just busywork. The consequence or impact of actions, behaviors, or habits is where real value resides.

Impact and consequences. Here is where the real value of work becomes apparent, particularly from the perspective of sponsors and supporters—those people funding projects. These are the measures in the system and organization records that reflect ultimate outcomes of work. You have likely heard them referred to as key performance indicators (KPIs). Measures of output, quality, and time are KPIs of importance to project funders. These measures are easily converted to money, making value evident or tangible. Other measures such as image, collaboration, and teamwork, are also important. These measures are more difficult to convert to money and represent intangible measures of success. Value may be inherently known, but much less obvious than the improvement in tangible measures. Tangible and intangible indicators of value are great—but they, too, are not always enough for some to describe the real value of your work.

It was worth it. Now, we are getting somewhere. Answering the question, "Is it worth it?" defines ultimate value. It answers the ROI question. Did we get more bang out of the buck than we put into it? How do benefits compare to costs? ROI informs our decisions daily. When we purchase an item, we ask ourselves, *Is it worth it? Am I going to get more benefit (tangible or intangible) by spending my money this way, than I would by holding on to it or spending it another way?* From a financial perspective, if benefits exceed costs, the project or activity is successful.

Defining success can be difficult if you are only looking through a single lens. Perspective is important. Demonstrating value from multiple perspectives will help prevent other people from undervaluing what you do.

FIVE LEVELS OF SUCCESS

Think about your projects. Without you, your team, their time, and financial resources, the project would never get off the ground. Therefore, value commences with the right people at the right time with the right amount of time available and the appropriate financial resources. From there, the project rolls out. To create and demonstrate your projects' real value, measure their success along the five categories in the previous section. Let's call them levels, recognizing the desire to take it to the next level. From the perspective of the funder or sponsor of the project, the next level is more valuable than the previous level. Here are the five levels of success, which define value for your project.

1. Reaction and Planned Action

Can you imagine working with a group of people who are uninterested, see no value in the project they are working on, and are uncommitted? The effort to get things moving would be tremendous. Creating value from a project requires that participants view the project as relevant to their situation, important to their success, and necessary to the success of others. Measuring reaction data will show you that the project is useful, helpful, and appropriate—with project participants committing to make the project successful. Perhaps they would even recommend it to others. Reaction data is an important first level of success.

2. Learning

People can only perform if they have the necessary information and know how to perform. Learning is the second level of success. But they must first buy in to the project. Learning can lead to buy-in. So, there is a connection between this second level of success and the previous. When people know what they need to know to make a project successful, their resistance will more than likely decrease, motivation will increase, and confidence to do the work will grow. To top it off, they can do the job! In most situations, projects include learning new knowledge and skills.

Measuring learning for your project is essential, even if done informally.

3. Application and Implementation

But it's not just about knowing; it's also about doing. Applying new skills, testing new concepts, completing tasks, exploring options, and identifying possibilities represent the third level of success—application and implementation. Measures taken here are helpful because they indicate that people are making progress using newly acquired knowledge, skills, and information. Those who are successful deliver greater value than those who are not. Application and implementation measures consider all processes and procedures that are necessary to make a project successful, such as tasks, actions, behaviors, checklists, and policies. The information you garner from this third level of success is powerful. It will tell you what is working, what is not, and what reinforcement and support you and your team need to move progress along.

4. Impact

So what if people are applying what they learn? How is it helping you improve output, quality, cost, and time? Sound familiar? This mighty question, or something similar, is the question for which our clients most frequently seek our advice. We make the connection between what people are doing and the consequence of their doing it. This delivers the outcomes we define as impact, the fourth level of success. Impact is the most important level of success from the perspective of sponsors and project funders. Impact measures represent the consequence of application and implementation—they are the strategic and operational KPIs.

This level of success includes improvements in measures such as revenue, new customers, productivity, quality, incidents, waste, retention, and time, to name a few. Indicators of these measures are in organization records and databases. In governments, nongovernmental organizations (NGOs), and nonprofits, impact may include patient outcomes, employment, graduation rates, infant mortality rates, addictions, crime rates, and poverty reduction. In addition to these tangible measures, there are also intangible measures such as customer satisfaction, image, stress, patient satisfaction, teamwork, quality of life, and alliances.

When you demonstrate the value of what you do at Level 4 Impact, you are getting to the heart of the issue that led you to do the work you are doing. Delivering impact relies on success throughout the journey, making measurement at the previous levels even more important. You can only improve the all-important KPIs with your project if people see the project as an imperative, know what they need to know, and do what they need to do to make the project successful.

5. Return on Investment

Is it worth it? In the end, for many projects, this is the bottom-line question. The return on investment in a project is the fifth and ultimate level of success. While there are many measures that tell us the financial efficacy of an investment, the two most common measures (and the most adaptable) are the benefit-cost ratio (BCR) and return on investment (ROI) as a percentage.

First, the benefit-cost ratio (BCR) is the monetary benefits from a project divided by the cost of the project. Benefit-cost analysis has been used for centuries and is meaningful to many executives, particularly those in nonprofits, governments, and NGOs.

The second measure is the ROI, expressed as a percentage. The formula compares the net benefits divided by the cost multiplied by 100. The net benefits are the monetary benefits minus the project costs. Derived from the finance and accounting field, the ROI formula is a common measure in businesses. Even consumers understand it, as they can clearly see ROI when they invest their money in a savings account with a financial institution. For most executives, it shows the efficient use of funds. Impact alone is one thing; knowing how the monetary value of your project compares to how much you spent on the project is another. The higher the ROI, the more efficient the use of the funds.

IF THESE LEVELS ARE SO LOGICAL,
WHY DON'T WE ALWAYS FOLLOW THEM?

The five levels of success offer a logical, rational approach to showing value. It's a classic logic model that dates to the 1800s. Most people agree, yet so few live it when planning projects, measuring success, and making adjustments.

Think about leadership. Probably no other subject has been the basis of so many books. People write about leadership again and again and again. Still, there is a big question, "What's the value of leadership?"

It's often said that a successful leader is someone who inspires others to dream more, learn more, do more, and become more. People react to successful leaders in a positive way. They respect the leader, and they are excited to work with the leader. A successful leader is someone people learn from—or the leader at least inspires them to learn. More importantly, a successful leader influences people to act and do more. Finally, a successful leader inspires people to become more—to contribute more—to have an impact. And this leader-follower journey should be worth it for the leader to lead and the follower to follow. That's the ROI. Do you see the logic in the levels? Table 2 profiles the concept.

Too often, we focus on one of these levels, stick with it, and that's it. You are looking for a charismatic leader, and that's all you want. Or maybe you're like a sponge and want to learn from a leader who is a great teacher, but that's it. Or you want a leader

Table 2. Success Profile of Leadership

Success Level	Leadership Qualities	Leadership Challenge	Leader Label	Leadership Evaluation
1	Admirable	Make it exciting	Charismatic	Reaction
2	Intelligence	Make it matter	Teacher	Learning
3	Bias for action	Make it stick	Influencer	Application
4	Results focus	Make it credible	Impactful	Impact
5	Value add	Make it worthwhile	Valuable	ROI

who will influence you to act—and nothing else. Maybe you want a leader who will influence you to make an impact, or a leader who creates a valuable experience for everyone. Realistically, a successful leader needs to be successful at all levels. Success at each level leads to success at the next.

Although these are logical levels, many individuals don't think in these terms. Sometimes this is because they view the different levels as too much information or too hard to deliver. Maybe they have felt the pain of taking the wrong measurements at each level, delivering less-than-valuable insights, so they opt out. These people fail to consider how this chain of value occurs. They also fail to consider the consequences that occur when their preferred level of success proves, well, unsuccessful. We need the different levels of success. They describe how we deliver ultimate value—and what we need to focus on when we don't.

SHOW THE VALUE PROCESS

You now have a framework of success measures that will help ensure you can report value from multiple perspectives. The next question you should be asking yourself is *How can I plan for, deliver, and capture these five levels of success for my project?* At the same time, you should be asking, *How do I ensure that the results I report are credible?* Like any journey, you need a road map (either paper or digital will work). This road map will help you explain to others what you are going to do, step by step. It also helps you explain what you did when it's done. The process presented in this book includes six steps to design, deliver, and evaluate a successful project, program, system, event, procedure, or initiative. Following the process will make your journey toward success much easier than if you just start out on your own because you think you know better than the cartographers. Our process is intentionally kept simple to give you flexibility when detours emerge. We will present the steps from the perspective of Doug Stewart from the opening story of this chapter.

Step 1: Why? Start with Impact

Back to the opening story. Following the workshop, Doug began thinking about the different measures important to the hospital system. One of the most important measures is patient length of stay (LOS). The longer a person stays in the hospital, the more it costs the hospital system and ultimately the patient. If the stay is extensive, healthcare reimbursement may not cover the hospital's costs. Monitoring LOS is particularly important for high-cost units, such as the intensive care unit (ICU). Doug decided to measure how a chaplain could influence LOS for the hospital. This became the "why" for his journey toward success.

Answering the question of why before moving forward with a project clarifies the impact you want from the project, program, or initiative. We're not talking about the aspiration or actions, activities, or behaviors. Rather, we mean the strategic or operational KPIs your project will improve. At this step, it is essential to align to key business measures that your work will influence and define the specific indicators. Ask, "Is this a problem worth solving or an opportunity worth pursuing?" If it is either, describe the problem or opportunity as precisely as possible as one or more business measures. Then, determine the current level of performance in the measure. This becomes your baseline.

Step 2: How? Select the Right Solution

Next, Doug reflected on the role chaplaincy plays in determining patient LOS. He anticipated, and research confirmed, that chaplaincy can improve LOS. Another important area of focus is improvement in patient satisfaction. When chaplains focus on patient satisfaction, the patients, and their family, cope better with the situation. Considering the work he and his fellow chaplains do and how it helps patients, Doug became convinced that good chaplaincy can improve the LOS measure.

This second step in the process answers the critical question: "Is this the right solution to influence the impact measure?" Answering this question may require some effort on your part or that of others. It certainly requires a mindset for curiosity. Interviews, focus groups, analytics, and phenomenological research can be helpful. However, you do not always need to go that far. Sometimes, enough insight can come from review of records, external studies, and benchmarking. In Doug's case, it was simply reflection on the work chaplains do and a few conversations.

To find your right solution, consider what is working and what needs to change. Change may include using a new procedure, new technology, new behavior, or taking specific corrective actions. Perhaps the change includes stopping something that is interfering with performance.

Determining the solution will generate new questions such as "What will people need to know to make the solution work?" Learning needs are important in finalizing the solution design and developing the evaluation strategy. Additionally, it is important to answer questions concerning how you or others prefer to implement the solution to address the need. Aligning the solution to the "why" and identifying what people need to know and how to best implement it serves as the basis for the project, described next, for Doug's situation.

Doug wanted to study patients who usually pass away in the ICU or are moved to a hospice level of care in the ICU. The place chaplains invest the most time in the ICU is with those most critical patients and patients who are at end of life. In the ICU, the chaplain is a key, trusted player in helping families come to terms with these challenging situations. Doug embedded a chaplain into the ICU; whereas before, the chaplain was a visitor and not part of the ICU team.

With Doug's project properly planned, he set out to demonstrate how the embedded chaplain can make a difference in LOS within the ICU. He compared the success of an ICU that had an embedded chaplain to another ICU without a chaplain embedded. While many factors can influence LOS in an ICU, Doug did the best he could to match the groups against those factors prior to measuring LOS. His thinking was that while he may not have a perfect match, the comparison would provide good enough insight to judge the contribution of chaplaincy.

Step 3: What? Expect Success with Objectives

Doug needed to set specific goals for his project to reduce length of stay, the impact objective. To achieve success with LOS, Doug knew he must also achieve success as the chaplain performs his work. So, Doug set application objectives that described how he would interact with the patient, family, and the team. Doug wanted to ensure that everyone, including the patient, followed the processes and protocols to carry out the spiritual care work. To ensure success, he also knew people needed to know what he was doing and their role in making chaplaincy successful. So, he set learning objectives. Finally, Doug knew that everyone involved must see the chaplain's work as relevant to the situation, important to better health care, something they will make successful, and a process they would recommend to others. He, therefore, set objectives that clarified the reactions he hoped to receive from others in the process.

This third step in the journey sets expectations for success along the way. This provides direction, so that everyone involved knows exactly what they need to do to improve performance in measures that matter. To be successful here, you need to:

1. Establish the definition of success recognizing that success does not occur until the impact occurs. This concept is important because we sometimes prematurely think success comes from learning or application. No, the project

is not successful until there is a demonstrable impact. In Doug's case, this was reducing length of stay.

2. Define objectives for reaction, learning, application, and impact because objectives provide focus, direction, and guidance. They serve as the blueprint for designing and delivering the project and measuring success at all four levels.

3. Share the objectives with others involved in the project, so they will know what to do to make the project successful. Each person involved in the project works to achieve the desired success at the impact level. They are designing for impact.

Step 4: How Much? Collect Data along the Way

Doug executed the project, and along the way he captured reaction data and learning data to determine the likelihood of successful improvement in LOS. Although informal, his data collection included journaling his observation of people's reactions, learning, and insights. Collecting the application data involved a slightly more formal documentation that everyone was doing their part to ensure a successful intervention and that patients were on track for an appropriately timed discharge from the hospital. Finally, he collected impact data by monitoring the length of stay for his unit.

This fourth step captures the data on the first four levels of success. Demonstrating the evolution of success as a project is underway is an essential step in this process. It is important for you to collect reaction data early to determine if those involved in the project see its value. Whether formally or informally, you must collect learning data to ensure that everyone knows what they should do to drive success. Capture application data to see if people are using what they have learned, and that they are doing this frequently and consistently. Finally, collect impact data on the measures selected at the beginning of the project.

Step 5: What's It Worth? Analyze the Data

With data showing improvement in LOS for the ICU with an embedded chaplain, Doug compared it to the measure of LOS to the control group—the ICU without an embedded chaplain. He saw very little improvement in LOS in the control group, but more improvement in the experimental group. The difference between the two groups proved to be significant. Doug reviewed the two groups again to make sure that he was comparing similar groups. He asked himself and others on his team, "Is there anything in these groups that would affect this measure or any differences between these groups that would affect the measure?" Doug convinced himself that no other major influence could be affecting the groups, giving him confidence that his claim about how much improvement was due to the embedded chaplain. This step is essential to the credibility of his claim that good chaplaincy improves LOS.

When analyzing data, credibility is a key concern. This step of the process determines if the impact data will be tangible or intangible and calculates the fifth level of success, ROI. While impact data provide evidence that the work made a difference, more compelling proof is required. This step sorts out the effects of the project on the impact data, recognizing that not all the improvement is the result of this project. Some of it may come from other influences internally or externally. This step will help you credibly back up your claim that the project has an impact.

Doug wanted to show the actual ROI. He located the costs for each day of stay in ICU. He extrapolated the impact findings for one year and multiplied the number of days avoided by the cost for a one-day stay in the hospital. This yielded a savings of $251,640 (monetary benefits). Doug then examined the cost of the chaplain on the project, which was $33,800. He calculated the return on investment, which compares the monetary benefits to the costs of the chaplaincy. The project realized a very high ROI:

$$ROI = \frac{\text{Project Benefits} - \text{Project Costs}}{\text{Project Costs}} \times 100$$

$$ROI = \frac{\$251{,}640 - \$33{,}800}{\$33{,}800} \times 100 = 644.5\%$$

For every dollar invested in this project, the dollar is returned, plus an additional $6.45. Chaplaincy proved to be well worth the investment.

Sometimes it is important to address the question, "What's it worth?" To do this requires you to convert the impact to a monetary value and calculate the costs of the work. Using these two numbers you can then calculate the ROI, which will tell you in numerical terms if the project is worth the investment in it.

Step 6: So What? Leverage the Results

The final step in Doug's journey was to present the results to show the value of this project and its worth to the hospital and the profession. Doug pointed out that this project was a win-win-win project: (1) the appropriate care for the patient; (2) better care for the families of the patients as they go through the patient's terminal condition; (3) cost savings for the hospital. Clearly, the results were impressive, and this study helped him obtain the continued, needed support, and, yes, funding from the hospital administrator. Today, Doug shares his journey with other chaplains by speaking at conferences and writing in professional journals. He has even won awards for this project. Doug did what many will not—demonstrate the real value of his work, chaplaincy. In doing so, he inspired others in the chaplaincy field to show the value of what they do. It is worth the effort from all perspectives.

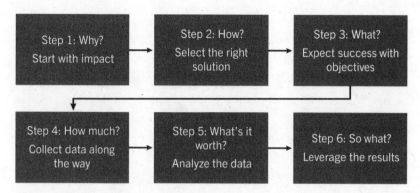

Figure 1. The Show the Value Process Model

When the ROI is determined, the question becomes "So what?" The critical issue now is to leverage the results for maximum benefit. The goal is always to make the outcome better. If the project is successful, make it more successful. If it is not successful, change things to make it successful the next time or make the next project successful. Use the results to gain support, commitment, influence, and funding.

The road map for your journey toward value is shown in Figure 1. This book devotes a chapter to each step. These steps are simple, easy to use, and will not consume excessive amounts of time. Following the six steps will provide you with credible answers to questions frequently asked about your work: Why? How? What? How much? What's it worth? and So what?

WHAT HAPPENS WHEN RESULTS ARE SURPRISING?

Katie Westwood led the tuition assistance program at a large Fortune 50 company. Many employees used the tuition refund program to take evening or online courses. It was a popular benefit, but the senior management felt the tuition refund program should be a retention factor that would keep people at the organization. The company had a great benefits package, excellent pay, and great working conditions. There was minimal turnover, and retention was not an issue. Top executives had made comments that the tuition refund program should possibly be discontinued because it was not affecting turnover.

Katie knew about these discussions and was concerned because she felt there were benefits to having the tuition refund, many of them intangible. Katie took on a project to show the program's value and conducted a study with the participants of the tuition refund program. She collected data directly from the participants to measure their perceived value of the program and get a sense of the skills, competencies, and knowledge they had gained and the extent to which they use what they learned on the job or in career moves.

Katie also collected impact data, which showed that there was little or no connection to turnover. The tuition refund benefit was not much of a factor in retaining employees. However, it was a factor in improving career mobility and career enhancement. As it turned out, career mobility was a high-value measure to the organization. In fact, at the time of the study and today, the company celebrates the fact that the former president started on the front line of the organization. Even Katie began as a frontline worker. Through the tuition refund program, she obtained a bachelor's degree, a master's degree, and her doctorate. The program enabled her to progress in her career and manage the tuition assistance program. Later, she became the director of leadership development.

Katie presented the data to the management team. She detailed how the program was working and the fact that it was not driving retention. She explained that if the program value was based on its connection to turnover, the ROI would be negative. However, it was responsible for much of the internal career mobility and career development with many promotions and transfers linked to the program. Katie had difficulty placing a monetary value on those promotions and transfers but knew that it probably could be done with extra effort and even offered to do so.

Her presentation made the executives realize that the program was adding value, and they decided not to discontinue it. They also decided to change the program design to help employees in their work by focusing on selected majors or job-related courses that were specific to the organization. This adjustment provided more focus on career opportunities and career mobility. Essentially, this study, completed at the impact level with a negative ROI, prevented the executives from taking negative action. It saved the tuition refund program from possible discontinuation or severe restriction.

Are you afraid your work will not demonstrate extremely positive returns? Don't be. Disappointing results do not always translate into discontinuation of a project or reprimand by the boss. Intangible benefits can be strong enough to make up the difference. Even if the impact is disappointing, the opportunity is there to understand what led to disappointment. Essentially, even if a program lacks financial value, the consequences may not be a problem. Because you have the foresight to collect all the other data, you can use it to determine what caused the financial failure. The changes necessary to lead to success are usually obvious. Thus, having negative results at Level 4 Impact or Level 5 ROI doesn't mean that your project, you, or your team will be terminated. It merely means you have an opportunity to adjust. Of course, if results indicate that you implemented the wrong solution at the outset, well, maybe you don't need that solution after all.

SHOW THE VALUE THINKING

When you begin to use the five levels of success and the six steps of the Show the Value Process to deliver that value, your thinking completely changes. Previously, we mentioned changing your mindset; now it's time to be specific. When you begin to work with this process, you approach your projects and your work differently. Show the Value thinking includes these issues:

1. Take action before someone asks for results.
2. Respect the value chain for the five levels of success.
3. Remember that the most important measure of success is impact.
4. Start with the end in mind.
5. Design for the results that you need.
6. Use ROI analysis selectively.
7. Look for the positive in a negative ROI.

When you begin thinking this way, you'll never go back to the traditional approach of evaluating your projects and initiatives.

HOW TO USE THIS BOOK

This book is based on almost three decades of research and practice. We (the authors, our team, and the users of the Show the Value Process) have measured the success of individuals involved in leadership development, coaching, team building, communication, empowerment, and a variety of different self-help processes. We have measured the success of habits, behaviors, culture, actions, networking, collaboration, and other hard-to-measure items. And, of course, we measure the success of technology, quality, marketing, and even work itself. Our combined experience is distilled into the six logical steps described in this chapter. We invite you to explore these steps in more detail, with more real-world examples in the remaining chapters.

Our approach to measurement is a proven process that places success on different levels. Each level adds to your work's profile of success and in the end describes a complete journey toward value. Higher levels of measures provide more compelling evidence of contributions, although each of the lower levels is essential. The concept is unique, novel, and effective. The Show the Value Process, in six steps, plans for the success levels, captures and analyzes the success levels, and leverages the results of the success levels.

The Show the Value Process described in this chapter offers a logical way to deliver value meaningful to those who matter to you and the project. It requires you to begin a project with the end in mind to ensure that your approach is the right fit, given the problem or opportunity you and your organization face. It requires you to define specific, measurable objectives and to use those objectives as the framework for designing your work. Then, you collect data throughout project implementation and analyze the data along the five levels of success. Finally, the process requires that you present and use the results to demonstrate value and to influence process improvement and funding.

That sounds like a lot, doesn't it? Well, maybe not. Just keep this in mind: It's a logical, credible process that is easy to follow and use. The next six chapters examine the six steps in more detail with tips, tools, stories, examples, applications, and encouragement. You will learn how to start your project, set precise objectives, collect all types of data, convert data to money, and calculate ROI. Read on!

NEXT STEPS

Now that you see the process, here are the actions to take:

1. **Review the website.** This will allow you to see what is available to you, how it can help you, and when you might need to reference it as you measure the success of your project.
2. **Identify your project.** Many of you had a project in mind when you purchased this book. Others were just curious. Still, for others, the project that you had in mind is probably not the right one you want to evaluate, now that you

have been introduced to the process. The key is to identify a project that you want to evaluate along the five levels of success, so that you can show the value of what you do.

3. **Find a sponsor.** When the results of your evaluation are in, you want to share them with someone. The most important person is the sponsor. The sponsor is the person who cares about this project and whose support is important to you. This may be the person who funds it, approves it, or asks you to implement it. For every project, there is someone who has an interest. This is the person with whom you will share results.

4. **Read the next chapter.** The next chapter begins the first of the six steps, starting with why.

CHAPTER 2

Why? Start with Impact

MYTH: It's almost impossible to connect most projects to
business needs.

REALITY: Essentially, every project can be connected to a
business need.

Chip Huth, the new leader of a SWAT team in the Kansas City, Missouri, Police Department, knew what he had to do. Citizen complaints against the team were excessive, averaging about 30–40 per year. They were also expensive, costing the department an average of $70,000 per complaint just for the investigations. The deputy chief (DC) who appointed Chip was clear—Chip needed to "clean up" the mess. The DC was concerned about optics from the complaints and the many irritations they were causing.[1]

Expectations were vague, and the accepted remedy was potentially a "house cleaning" and subsequent creation of a new team. Chip knew what he was facing. He accepted the assignment because he loved working in teams. Initially, Chip didn't believe the team could be "fixed." Admittedly, Chip was completely self-centered in his thinking and simply loved the thrill of the work. He reassured the DC that he could whip the team into shape (not believing anyone could do so) and initially sought token improvements by addressing problem behaviors.

Unexpectedly, through a series of personal and professional encounters, Chip was exposed to a personal improvement process called Outward Mindset from the Arbinger Institute. Arbinger's research indicates that people operate at any given time from one of two mindsets: an inward mindset or an outward mindset. When operating with an inward mindset, you focus only on your own goals and objectives without considering your impact on others. With an outward mindset, however, you see others as people who matter as much as you do. You consider their needs, challenges, and objectives. And you focus on collective results.

As Chip began applying the Outward Mindset framework to each area of his life, including his leadership responsibilities with the team, it seemed logical that this could impact the team. Although Chip was not certain that the Outward Mindset would deliver fewer complaints or build a better relationship with the community, he was willing to give it a try.

He introduced the team to this process. When they were exposed to it, they responded positively. The team asked Chip to lead them in applying the Outward Mindset skills and framework, in role-modeling the behaviors, and showing them that it works. That was all Chip needed. He had the business measure, citizen complaints at roughly $70,000 each, the right solution, Outward Mindset, and the right people at the right time. He was ready to go.

THE PROJECT BEGINS WITH THE END IN MIND

There is something to be said for the adage, begin with the end in mind. Knowing where you are going will certainly get you there faster. In this chapter, we begin with Step 1 in the Show the Value Process: Start with Impact. Impact describes *Why* you are taking on the work or project you are pursuing.

Demonstrating impact due to a project is important. It is what top executives want to see. Impact to them is improvement in measures of output, quality, cost, and time, as well as customer satisfaction, job satisfaction, teamwork, and innovation. Executives want to see a positive consequence from what people do with what they know.

The same can be said of donors to nonprofits. Donors give money because they identify with the mission of the organization.

They want to know that their investment in the nonprofit is having an impact—that it is improving the lives of others and the communities it serves.

Innovators and entrepreneurs want to deliver impact. When the developers of the Uber app started the project, they had three impact measures in mind: 1) quicker rides (a measure of time) compared to a classic taxi; 2) cheaper rides (a measure of cost) compared to a classic taxi; and 3) better customer experience (a measure of quality) than that offered by a classic taxi.[2] These three impact measures were their guiding light. And good news for all of us riders, they achieved their goals in almost all cities where they operate.

Impact can represent problems to be solved or opportunities to pursue. For example, Chip Huth's assignment at the Kansas City SWAT team was based on a problem described by impact data. There were too many citizen complaints, and that problem needed to be corrected. In contrast, Uber did not necessarily set out to correct a problem, but rather to take advantage of an opportunity—to deliver a faster, cheaper, and better rider experience than riders were having with classic taxicab services.

In both situations, project owners knew why they were doing what they were doing. They knew the impact they wanted to achieve before their projects got off the ground. Knowing the answer to the question "Why?" before you ever launch into your work will help ensure that you create and demonstrate value. In answering the question, you will determine:

- The impact you hope to achieve by addressing problems or opportunities, and
- The value that achieving the impact can deliver.

DEFINE IMPACT

Success with achieving impact first depends on the meaning of the word "impact." Precisely defining the measure of impact and knowing the baseline begins the setup of the aim for your project. It is first important to know the nature of impact measures. Some measures are more quantifiable than others; these are what we refer to as hard measures. Those that are less quantifiable are considered soft measures. Both can be equally important in demonstrating the value of your work. Let's look a little deeper.

Hard versus Soft Impact Measures

Impact measures comprise both hard data and soft data. Table 3 shows examples of hard data, those objective measures that are easier to convert to money and that most organizations monitor.[3] You can find them in operating reports, as key performance indicators (KPIs), and on scorecards and dashboards. Output, quality, cost, and time are the foundation of work. Every team member in an organization strives to deliver on these four types of measures. Output is the production of the work. Production can be revenue-generating output (e.g., sales of new products), manufactured output (e.g., cars built), or process output (e.g., claims processed). Quality measures are those that indicate the work meets a certain standard of excellence and can be expressed as errors, waste, and rework. Time measures are those that indicate duration or amount of time, typically measured in minutes, hours, days, etc. Costs are, well, costs—the monetary impact to the organization when something occurs. These measures also roll up into aggregate measures important to higher-level reporting to management and senior executives.

Soft measures, such as those shown in Table 4, are subjective in nature and more difficult to convert to money. However, progress is being made in this area. In today's era of analytics, soft measures are more meaningful than in the past, and this often translates into monetary value. Still, in most organizations, many of these measures remain intangible yet are still important. Intangible measures are those you cannot credibly convert to money within a reasonable amount of time. Improving intangible measures may be the sole purpose of your project, and that's okay.

Table 3. Examples of Hard Data

Output	Time
Citizens vaccinated	Length of stay
Graduation rate	Cycle time
Placement rate	Equipment downtime
Units produced	Overtime
Income increased	On-time shipments
Production	Project time
Money collected	Processing time
Licenses issued	Supervisory time
New accounts generated	Time to proficiency
Forms processed	Time to graduate
Loans approved	Repair time
Inventory turnover	Time to replace
Criminals prosecuted	Response time
Inspections made	Late times
Patients X-rayed	Lost time days
Projects completed	Wait time
Jobs secured	
Patients discharged	
Criminals captured	Quality
Shipments	Readmissions
	Failure rates
	Dropout rates
Costs	Scrap
Budget variances	Waste
Unit costs	Rejects
Costs by account	Error rates
Variable costs	Rework required
Fixed costs	Shortages
Overhead costs	Product defects
Operating costs	Deviations from standard
Accident costs	Product failures
Program costs	Inventory adjustments
Incarceration costs	Infections
Shelter costs	Incidents
Treatment costs	Compliance discrepancies
Participant costs	Agency fines
Cost per day	Accidents
	Crime rate

Table 4. Examples of Soft Data

Leadership	*Client Service*
Teamwork	Client complaints
Collaboration	Client satisfaction
Networking	Client dissatisfaction
Communication	Client impressions
Alliances	Client loyalty
Decisiveness	Client retention
Caring	Client value
Compassion	Clients lost
Work Climate/Satisfaction	*Employee Development/Advancement*
Grievances	Promotions
Discrimination charges	Capability
Employee complaints	Intellectual capital
Job satisfaction	Programs completed
Organization commitment	Transfers
Employee engagement	Performance appraisal ratings
Employee loyalty	Readiness
Intent to leave	Development assignments
Stress	
Initiative/Innovation	*Image/Reputation*
Creativity	Brand awareness
New ideas	Reputation
Suggestions	Impressions
Trademarks	Social responsibility
Copyrights and patents	Environmental friendliness
Process improvements	Social consciousness
Partnerships	Diversity/inclusiveness
	External awards

Obvious and Not-So-Obvious Impact

In addition to the measures being both hard and soft, knowing what specific impact measures to target can be obvious and, then again, not so obvious. The most obvious measures are those KPIs you monitor routinely to know how well you and your team are performing. Others are found in quarterly and annual reports as well as benchmarking reports you use to compare your organization's performance to that of competitors or similar organizations. Through these reports, you will gain insights as to the direction in which the organization is moving, how your organization is faring in comparison to competitors or similar organizations, and what hurdles it faces in achieving its goals. If you support other functions or if you are an external consultant, a conversation with your client will also lead to recognizable issues.

For example, if you are a claims processor, you may have noticed that in your organization, the time to process a disability claim has increased 30 percent in two years. That's a clear problem. By correcting it, the impact would be a reduction in time to process a disability claim. Or maybe you manage a call center, and you have just received a report from the benchmark companies in your industry. The typical absenteeism rate for other call centers is 5.4 percent, whereas the absenteeism rate for your call center is 12.3 percent. This is both a problem and an opportunity. By addressing it, the impact will be a reduction in absenteeism.

In contrast, however, the impact of a problem or opportunity may not be so clear. For example, an opportunity may exist for the organization to provide jobs for autistic young adults. But why? What specific impact will occur? Is it to reduce the number of unemployed autistic young adults? Or fill a job gap in a specific department? Is it to enhance diversity metrics? Maybe the impact has to do with corporate social responsibility and will lead to recognition by employees, customers, shareholders, and the community. Or perhaps the impact is simply to increase the number of autistic young adults employed because it supports the organization's mission.

Or maybe there is an opportunity for the organization to become a "green" organization. While the ambition may be admirable, two questions follow. First, "Why do we want to become green?" Maybe it is to gain more customers, attract a different type of talent, or because it is the right thing to do. The second question asks, "What measures need to improve that will indicate whether we are moving toward that goal?" Answers may include reduction in solid waste, carbon emissions, or megawatt-hours used. Answers could also include customer perception, employee experience, or recognition on industry reports.

Not-so-obvious problems and opportunities often stem from executive aspirations, news articles, or shifts in shareholder interests. These ambitions are important and often valuable, but defining their impact may take some work. Consider the journey of Paula Patel, a systems coordinator for a technology company.

Since the COVID-19 pandemic, Paula Patel has been working remotely, and it's working out well for her. She has felt more in control of her work, more satisfied with her work-life balance, and her stress levels are down. She avoids the previous long commute and the additional expense of working at the office. Paula feels that she's been more productive, and her boss seems to agree. She's even worked extra hours and made extra efforts to collaborate with her team to ensure the work-at-home arrangement is successful.

Unfortunately, the company executives have asked employees to return to the office at least in some type of hybrid arrangement. However, the executives have agreed to hear employees out. If employees can make a sound business case, they will be allowed to continue their remote work arrangement. Paula considered leaving, but now she wants to make a business case for working at home.

Paula begins thinking about presenting data describing the ROI of remote work to the company, for herself personally, the environment, and the community. Paula reviews actual studies and finds measures that have been influenced by work-at-home solutions, such as productivity, retention, office expenses, and unplanned absenteeism.[4] Retention is a measure related to her decision to continue to work for the company. The fact that she doesn't want to return to the office and would probably leave if she was forced to return, a turnover is prevented. That's a big expense for the company.

Measuring productivity will be a little tricky for her because her work doesn't necessarily produce output, such as processing claims or investigating customer complaints. So she may have to measure her productivity subjectively rather than objectively, using an actual countable unit.

Paula knows the company can save a lot of money by giving up her office and using it for other purposes or other employees as the company grows—this could lead to a positive ROI. While there are some expenses the company incurs for her working at home, they are minimal. So, just by avoiding the office expenses alone, the remote work arrangement would deliver a high ROI from the company's perspective.

In addition to the benefits to the company, Paula thought about the ROI from her perspective. The measures are largely intangible. They include work-life balance, stress reduction, job satisfaction, convenience, and less expense. Of course, she would have to deal with the lack of social interaction and work hard on teamwork, engagement, and collaboration.

From the environmental perspective, remote work reduces carbon emissions. She could probably calculate this down to the reduction of tons emitted into the environment each year. Paula knows the company is interested in helping the environment, so this should be a good measure. Finally, from the community perspective, city and county officials are always concerned about traffic and congestion and promote remote working.

With all these impact measures detailed, Paula is ready to embark on the study to show the value of working remotely from these three perspectives.

When your impact measures are not so obvious, one way to approach defining them is to consider what would happen if you did not address the problem or take advantage of the opportunity. In Paula's situation, if executives were to call off the work-at-home arrangement altogether, Paula:

- Would likely leave (turnover),
- Would cost the company more for her office (office expenses),
- Wouldn't accomplish as much (productivity),

- Would be back on the road (carbon emissions),
- Would spend more money (personal expenses),
- Would be stressed out, and job satisfaction would decrease (the intangibles)

By asking yourself or your client the question, "What happens if we do nothing?" the impact measures will usually surface.

Baseline Performance

After you define the measure, capture the baseline performance. Because you are doing work that will add value, you will need to know your starting point so that you can evaluate against it after the work is done. Where do you find baseline? Typically, you will note baseline in the same records from which you define the impact measures. This is true whether the measure is considered hard data or soft data. Operational KPI performance, including customer and employee experience data, is typically obvious. For measures that are less obvious, subjective techniques for establishing baseline may be necessary.

Take Paula, in our earlier story. One benefit of her working at home is that she is more productive. How does Paula define productivity? Even she admits that measuring the productivity of her work is tricky. She could measure her productivity using time on tasks and in meetings. Thanks to technology, we have an app for that. The challenge for Paula, however, is that she may not have used an app to track her time prior to working at home. If that is the case, she can estimate baseline time on productive work using her calendar and other notes. Another approach may be for Paula to indicate her perception of productivity prior to working at home using Likert-type response choices (i.e., disagree-agree) on a series of survey questions.

For most impact measures, a baseline will likely exist. If it does not, there is a way to get there. Measurement is a balance between accuracy and cost and art and science.

The Monetary Value of Problems and Opportunities

You now know the problem or opportunity that lies ahead. You also know the impact you are trying to achieve and the baseline for the impact measures. A final consideration when clarifying the why of your project is to determine the magnitude of the problem or opportunity—basically, answering the question, "Is this problem or opportunity worth pursuing?" Answering this question is most effectively done by converting the impact measures to money and multiplying by the current performance in the measure. For example, in the case of Chip Huth and the Kansas City SWAT team, the impact measure of interest was citizen complaints. They were averaging 30–40 per year at the cost of $70,000 each just for the investigations. The problem cost the police department $2,100,000 to $2,800,000 annually—just for the investigation! Knowing the monetary value put the complaint problem under a much brighter light.

History shows that the idea of monetizing problems and opportunities is not new. Think of all the things on which monetary value has been placed: parks, bridges, dams, green space, water quality, damage to buildings, recidivism, health and wellness, employee engagement, customer satisfaction, library usage, chaplaincy, and the list goes on.

Why monetary value? Money is the generally accepted medium of exchange, and because it is numerical, it is subject to mathematical analysis. Plus, it is something we all understand. When we convert problems and opportunities to money, we can compare them to determine which ones are the worthiest pursuits (taking into consideration the intangibles, of course). Monetizing problems is of particular interest when the aim is to demonstrate the ROI of a project. If you plan to demonstrate impact only, you don't necessarily need the monetary value. However, when possible, it is a good practice to determine monetary value because it makes for a compelling conversation with executives and clients. We will show you how to convert measures to monetary value in Chapter 6.

Anna Chen, an entrepreneurial-focused teacher, explored the opportunity to provide empowerment training for seventh and eighth grade students. She wanted to motivate her students to be more accountable. But, as she thought about it, she wondered what would it mean if they were better team members. Taking responsibility for their actions? Setting goals? Being model students? This opportunity quickly led her to some potential impacts. She anticipated that they would attend school more often and have fewer absences. They would have better grades, and more students would be promoted to the next grade. They would have fewer disciplinary discussions, and they would have fewer incidents of tardiness.

As Anna continued to think this through to the next step, she realized these were costly issues for the school system. When a student is absent in many school systems, the school doesn't receive funding for that day because funding in many schools is based on attendance. Not being promoted to the next grade is also very costly. Additionally, the disciplinary discussions have a cost because they require an investment in counselors. Anna realized that by exploring this opportunity, there were many potential impacts and a real possibility of a large payoff.[5]

CAPTURE VALUE BEFORE BEING ASKED

As you read this chapter, are you thinking to yourself, *No one is asking for this type of data, so I will wait until they do*? If you are, stop. Here's why. Waiting until a client or senior leader asks for the data is usually too late. Read what happened with Sarah Robertson.

Sarah Robertson provides counseling services at food banks in Canada. As a counselor for Catholic Family Services, she helps individuals with financial problems who cannot afford to pay for food.

Sarah helps them understand their situation and plots a path for improvement. Issues her clients face may include job loss, medical problems, family member addictions, or family member incarceration. Any of these can devastate the financial security of low- to middle-income families.

Sarah was surprised when a representative of the provincial government—which funds her program—visited her and asked about results. When Sarah asked for clarification on the kind of results, the representative asked, "Could you show the ROI of the counseling?"

Sarah was shocked and dismayed by the request. She had almost no data describing the value of her program except for the data she provided to the government indicating how many people were counseled, the type of counseling provided, and the number of counseling sessions conducted. Of course, she provided an invoice for her services. Beyond that, she had nothing.

About a month after the government visit, Sarah participated in the ROI Certification process offered through ROI Institute. Between the program content and discussions with her colleagues, she began to reach the conclusion that she may have more data than she thought—or at least ways to capture the data.

As part of the process, Sarah always develops an action plan with each person. The plan is based on the participants' situation, detailing what they must do to overcome their problem. In every case, there were specific actions that they must take, advice they should seek, other agencies they must visit, or employers where they should go for interviews. The point is that an action plan is in place to reach the impact. With some improvements and adjustments, she could easily use this information in reporting back to the government on the success people were having with the application of what they were learning.

Of most interest to the government was ROI. This meant that the impact data had to be converted into money. She felt comfortable that these values were available and could be obtained with minimal effort. In addition to the monetary benefits, Sarah had to account for her program's costs. Obviously, the government's fees for counseling represent the cost to the government, but that is not all. There was also the cost of the counseling room because, after all, the government is furnishing the facility. All the costs, indirect and direct, would need to be included, which she said should be not that difficult. Then the ROI calculation could be developed to meet the government request.

In addition to the impact measures and ROI, there were other intangible measures. If the counseling works, participants regain their self-esteem and dignity, family relationships are improved, and quality of life is enhanced. With all these measures in hand, Sarah concluded that she could have a complete set of data, measuring reaction, learning, application, impact, ROI, and the intangibles. This would provide the government the data it needed.

Unfortunately, before Sarah Robertson could complete her study, she received notice from the provincial government that her program had been canceled. She explained to the representative that she was working on an ROI study that should be completed in a month. The representative explained, "It's too late . . . The decision has been made. It was a difficult decision . . . But we must cut budgets. We just don't have the revenue, and we don't have any data about the success of this program."

Sarah was upset and angry. "How could the government be so cruel?" she asked. "Is everything about money?" She planned to challenge the decision but felt that it would probably be a waste of time. On top of this frustration was the reality that she must find another job. As an independent contractor, she must replace this lost contract with another one, and in this environment, it would be difficult. In addition, she worried about the people who come to the food bank. "Will someone be there to help them? Probably not," she concluded.

This is a sad but true story. The weight of not having data, broke Sarah's bridge. There are three issues. First, the counseling program was probably driving some important impacts, according to Sarah. If she had only been reporting impressive impact along the way, there likely would not have been an ROI request.

Second, just because the government did not ask for the data doesn't mean that she should not have been providing it. While Sarah did have to collect new data, her program was set up to do so for the most part.

Third, to ensure the best program and deliver the greatest results, funders should set an expectation that impact and ROI are important. Elevate the expectation to elevate the outcome.

So, there you have it. The first step in the Show the Value Process is to start with why and identify the specific impact measures that need to improve, so you know you are solving the problem or leveraging the opportunity in front of you. Impact measures may be hard or soft. You will find them in operations reports, databases, benchmark studies, and sometimes a simple conversation. Some measures and their baseline performance will be more obvious than others. When the impact is not so obvious, you may need to resort to a more determined effort to find the impact. To understand the true magnitude of the problem, convert your impact measures to money and multiply the value times the current performance in that measure. With impact and its value clearly in mind, you will now answer the question, "How?" by selecting the right solution.

NEXT STEPS

After completing this chapter, here are your action steps:

1. **Think about your project.** Is it solving a problem or taking advantage of an opportunity? Is it worth it? How do you know that? Answers to these questions will get you started correctly.
2. **Identify the specific business measures that need to be improved.** These measures are normally in the system and are often key performance indicators (KPIs). These measures are normally hard data. If not, they may be a combination of both hard and soft data.

3. **Visualize the process.** We provided a process with six logical steps. Think about your project and how it might unfold along these steps. Visualize success at each of the five levels and what it will take to ensure such success.

4. **Read the next chapter.** The next chapter focuses on finding the right solution.

CHAPTER 3

How? Select the Right Solution

MYTH: The solution to a problem is almost always obvious.

REALITY: The right solution is rarely obvious.

Ginger Luttrell spent 10 years as a software engineer, including configuration and programming at one of the world's largest business software companies. The intent of new systems implementations is to improve output, quality, cost, and time. Over the years of working with these systems implementations, she noticed a problem. When an implementation project would go live, end-users, those who worked in the business functional areas or departments, would ask questions such as:

Why did we spend money on software and implementation projects yet spend little on training and support for those who use the software?

Am I the only one who thinks the help desk isn't helpful?

Am I the only one who thinks that better system use will naturally lead to better business results?

How can we organize training and support without asking for a burdensome budget?

What do I need to learn to be a better user and to better help my colleagues?

Interestingly, end-users received comprehensive training on these systems during projects. Despite this fact, Ginger noticed that they experienced problems and frustrations on the job. As a result, productivity, quality, and time savings suffered rather than improved. The types of problems Ginger was addressing were universal. Additionally, some end-users would become so frustrated they would leave the company altogether. Ginger also saw that there was no channel for the voice of the end-users to get to the senior executives to address their issues and concerns.

Ginger began to realize a possible solution by addressing the precise business needs identified (productivity, quality, time, cost, and retention). The end-users needed a person who would support them on a routine basis. This person would serve as a mentor, coach, trainer, counselor, and trusted advisor to help them through complex implementation issues. This person is called a super user. At the same time, super users would help develop the end-users to become more valuable business team members—members with a broader vision and more complex skill sets, who could offer greater support in their organization.

Ginger realized that the cost of providing super users was much less than the savings that would be generated to make the software system more effective for the organization. She tested her theory in different organizations and was convinced that she had the right solution for the perplexing problem of large-scale systems implementation. Eventually, Ginger founded the Super User Network and now spends much of her time preparing and developing super users to perform this essential role in business departments worldwide.[1]

FINDING A SOLUTION

Knowing the why—the impact you are trying to achieve—is the first step. The next question is How do you achieve it? Many projects and programs begin because someone thinks these projects are the right solutions for a problem or opportunity. But are they?

For example, many of you likely remember when Starbucks shut down its stores for racial-bias training back in 2020—sparked by an event involving a Philadelphia Starbucks manager who had arrested two African American entrepreneurs. These two individuals had been waiting at the Starbucks for a business meeting. Starbucks hired SYPartners to deliver a three-and-a-half-hour racial-bias training to 175,000 employees in more than 8,000 Starbucks locations across the United States—all in the same day.[2]

It may have been good PR, and it certainly got attention, but did it solve the problem? Most of the research suggests that anti-bias training doesn't work. In fact, according to two researchers, "Hundreds of studies dating back to the 1930s suggest that anti-bias training does not reduce bias, alter behavior, or change the workplace."[3] So, how did Starbucks come to their solution to shut down stores and offer anti-bias training? Only the insiders know for sure. And, in all fairness, there are times when sending a strong message, as Starbucks did, is a worthy investment. Forgoing $12–14 million dollars in sales does communicate that company leaders recognize a problem when they see one. But what if no benefit comes from the investment? Can all organizations afford such an expensive gamble? How do you increase the chances of identifying the right solution?

There are many types of solutions to opportunities that we and our organizations face. Table 5 offers a sample of the solutions available to us.

Table 5. Typical Solutions

• Provide information/knowledge	• Initiate policy changes
• Build skills/competencies	• Implement process changes
• Install technology/systems	• Initiate job changes
• Implement procedures	• Provide rewards/recognition
• Organize meetings/events	• Offer tools/enablers

To increase the odds of selecting the right solution (and decrease the odds of selecting the wrong one), you will determine the:

- Performance that needs to change,
- Learning that supports the change, and
- Preferences that need to be met.

Let's explore these in more detail.

PERFORMANCE THAT NEEDS TO CHANGE

Performance that needs to change may include actions, processes, behaviors, procedural compliance, or even systems implementation. A gap in performance is the cause of the problem or the avenue to addressing an opportunity. Identifying the gap leads to the solution. Sometimes the performance that needs to change is easily recognizable, and, based on experience, you can quickly identify a feasible solution. If you recall, that's how Ginger Luttrell approached her problem. Her experience as a software engineer led her to create the role of super users to improve measures of productivity, quality, time, and retention often affected by large-scale systems implementation. Chip Huth, from Chapter 2, did the same. He took advantage of his experience with Outward Mindset to influence changes in the behavior of the Kansas City SWAT team when engaging with suspects and the community at large, to reduce citizen complaints.

On the other hand, there are times when your experience does not provide all the answers, so you must rely on the input of others. This is when it might be beneficial to converse with stakeholders or refer to case studies or benchmarking reports. The experience of others is often the best teacher. You might also take advantage of some of the analytical tools from problem solving, quality assurance, and performance improvement. Searching for multiple solutions is important since impact measures are often hindered for different reasons. When multiple solutions do evolve, it is important to decide whether to explore them as a whole or in priority order. This depends on the types of solutions, the cost of implementation, the extent to which the current system will support implementation, and the value of solving the problem. Rebecca Benson's use of nominal group technique led to the discovery of five different causes of turnover resulting in five different solutions.

Rebecca Benson is the vice president of human resources for a behavioral center with a mission to educate and treat individuals with autism, behavioral health disorders, and mental health illnesses. This nonprofit is steadfast in its efforts to help individuals reach their full potential and be productive members of society. The organization employs approximately 250 direct care staff who work with patients in the various facilities on the campus.

Rebecca was concerned about the high turnover rate among the direct care staff. Forty percent annual turnover is expensive and disruptive. Understanding the cause of this turnover was vital if she was going to solve the problem. It was easy for executives to assume pay was the issue. Their solution was to increase salaries. But Rebecca wondered if there were other issues more instrumental in the departure of direct care staff.

To explore the issue, Rebecca contracted an external consulting group to conduct focus groups with 50 direct care staff members, representing 20 percent of the entire team. Using nominal group technique (a structured brainstorming technique that identifies problems, generates solutions, and considers everyone's opinion in decision making), the consultants facilitated five focus groups with 10 staff members in each. No one from the leadership team in the nonprofit was involved with the focus groups.

The facilitator told focus group participants:

- The session's purpose was to explore why they think their colleagues are leaving;
- They were free to say whatever they wished;

- Any data or comments would be completely confidential, and again;
- The focus would be on why their colleagues were leaving.

In each session, the facilitator asked participants to create a list of why their colleagues were leaving the organization. Participants were given time to make their lists as complete as possible. Then, each person revealed a reason, one at a time, until the facilitator captured all reasons.

During the sessions, the facilitator noticed trust was building among participants as they would begin their sentences by saying, "I have a problem with . . ." To keep the group focused, the facilitators reminded participants that they were discussing their colleagues, not themselves, and that their input was appreciated.

Ultimately, the conversation revealed the true essence of what was occurring. By talking about their colleagues' reasons for leaving during the focus groups, the direct care staff told the facilitators indirectly why they would leave.

The facilitator listed the reasons on flip charts displayed around the conference room. A consolidation activity followed in which each reason was clarified, and similar reasons were combined. The facilitators then asked participants to examine the list and select the top five reasons their colleagues were leaving, placing each cause on an individual index card. Next, participants put their index cards in order based on the importance of the reason. They revealed the reasons one at a time, with each participant sharing their number-one reason. Five points were assigned to each number-one reason. Each number-two reason received four points, number-three reasons received three points, number-four reasons received two points, and number-five reasons received one point.

When the rankings were totaled, the item with the highest score was considered the number-one reason people left the organization. This process was repeated in each of the five focus groups. The results for the five groups were combined.

Combing the results for all focus groups produced the top five reasons why direct care staff left the organization.

1. Wages and benefits are low.
2. Quality of management is unacceptable.
3. More training and development is needed.
4. The nature of the work needs to be reviewed.
5. Scheduling of hours should be adjusted.

Low wages were the top reason. This was no surprise to Rebecca or others involved in the project. In addition to the low wages, Rebecca knew there were inconsistencies in how the pay system was being administered, so this problem would have to be handled quickly. The second was the quality of management. This was an unexpected insight. According to the focus groups, managers were not supportive, trusting, appreciative, motivating, or encouraging. This would lead to a new management training program.

Third, there was a need for more training and development. In some cases, focus group participants indicated there was no training. A need to update compliance training had also been brought up as a critical issue. The fourth issue concerned the job itself. Staff members were completely burned out. Some employees were uncomfortable with some of the duties they were performing. This required a review of and adjustments in the job. Finally, scheduling issues needed to be addressed to avoid excessive overtime and create more flexible working arrangements. Collectively, these five reasons accounted for 90 percent of the causes for employees to leave the organization.

With the top five issues identified, Rebecca and the team designed the solutions to address each one. Implementing each solution corrected the problems. The solutions reduced the turnover rate from about 40 percent to 21 percent, which represented tremendous cost savings for the organization.

Table 6. Diagnostic Tools

Tool	Use when
Affinity diagram process (aka, affinity chart, K-J Method, thematic analysis)	Confronted with many facts or ideas, issues seem too large and complex to grasp, group consensus is necessary
Analytics	Creating models to develop insights about the interaction between different data sources
Cause-and-effect diagrams (aka, fishbone diagram, Ishikawa diagram)	Identifying possible causes for a problem and when you want to move a team's thinking out of a rut
Engagement surveys	Assessing employees' levels of engagement or disengagement, how engagement compares across functions, predicting talent risks, and identifying opportunities for leadership growth
Exit interviews/surveys	Assessing the reasons people leave an organization
Focus groups	Exploring needs, thoughts, and perceptions of people when it is important for them to hear from other people
Force-field analysis	Analyzing the root cause of a problem by comparing the positive and negative forces, along with their relative strength, of a situation
Mind-mapping	Taking notes and summarizing discussions, brainstorming ideas, breaking down complex problems, and analyzing and processing information
Nominal group technique	Brainstorming using structure that gives every participant an opportunity to contribute, present their ideas, and prioritize their ideas and those of others using a point system
Probing interviews	Seeking information about assumptions and perceptions and when probing for details and lengthy explanations are important
Simulations	Conducting experiments on a real system or if a real setting is impossible or impractical
Social network analysis (aka organizational network analysis)	Investigating social structures within an organization to understand workflow, collaboration, knowledge sharing, dependencies on people, talent flight risks, work overload
Statistical process control	Monitoring process inputs, discovering issues in internal systems, and finding solutions for production issues
Statistical quality control	Monitoring process outputs, discovering issues in internal systems, and finding solutions for production issues

There is no one best technique to answer your performance needs question. How you answer the question depends on:

- The question itself,
- Reliability/validity of the tool and its output,
- Cost of using the tool,
- Convenience of using the tool, and
- Utility of the output.

Table 6 lists a few diagnostic tools that can help you identify performance needs and an appropriate solution.[4]

In a larger organization, with a huge opportunity, it may require some additional resources to make sure that it's the right solution. Here's an example taken from a telecom in Southeast China.

Xing Wang is the general manager of the Lincheng branch of National Telecom, Inc. Lincheng is the fifth-largest city of Handong Province in southeast China, which represents one of the high-potential markets of National Telecom. In 2018, Xing and his marketing team launched a marketing program to improve the branch's business performance. The project more than doubled the market share of smartphones in an important market segment within six months. This project not only won an award from National Telecom but also demonstrated the value-creation process of a marketing-performance improvement project. It satisfied the payoff and business needs of the organization by delivering increased sales revenue, improved customer satisfaction, and intangible benefits of better brand equity, and it enhanced client relationships. This project showed that even without investing significant additional resources, it is possible to improve marketing performance significantly with smart efforts and use of a proper methodology.

To ensure business alignment, they started the project with an organizational analysis by reviewing the corporate vision, mission, and goals. The corporate mission of connecting people with the world and the key organizational strategy to expand business scale required the Lincheng branch to continually increase its market share and service level in the mobile phone market. After completing the organizational analysis, they conducted situation analysis and examined the environmental factors, both inside and outside the organization, at the world, workplace, work, and worker levels. These analyses revealed multiple marketing performance gaps, including a market share gap in the top 500 enterprises market.

With the help of consultants, Xing and his team conducted a key value chain analysis, an analytical tool developed by Sinotrac Consulting Company in Beijing. The analysis identified the relatively low "effective employee contact rate" as a measure for improvement. The effective employee contact rate measures the ratio of the number of employees effectively contacted by National Telecom's marketing team and the total number of employees in an organization. On average, the effective employee contact rate was only 20 percent, which was significantly below the 50 percent target. The key value chain analysis showed that closing this gap would help the Lincheng branch achieve its market share goal of 20 percent. Xing and his team then conducted cause analysis using the behavioral engineering model (BEM) before considering multiple solutions to address this business measure and increase the effective employee contact rate. The cause analysis showed that the primary reasons for the low contact rate were (1) a lack of information about the organizational structure, employee characteristics, and needs; (2) a lack of resources and channels to communicate with the target employees; and (3) a lack of incentives to motivate channel partners for better coordination and cooperation. The team then designed a package of solutions, based on the causes, to close the gap.

This is an excellent example of a project that uncovered business needs (starting with why) and then taking steps to identify what was causing the initial failure to recognize business needs. The causes led to a solution.[5]

LEARNING THAT SUPPORTS THE CHANGE

Learning supports implementation of the solution. And there are a variety of people who will support the success of the solution. Therefore, identifying learning needs is essential. The question you are answering here is, "What do people need to know to do what we want them to do?" This "knowing" may include skills, information, or insight about others or oneself. It may include knowledge of people, places, events, or systems.

Determining learning needs can be as simple as asking the individuals involved, "What do you need to know to make the project successful?" Or it can be as complex as requiring knowledge assessments, demonstration of abilities, or other types of research and analysis. It is essential to ensure what people know, what they don't know, and how much effort it will take to get them where they need to be to make the project successful.

For example, Richard Coldwell, a traffic design coordinator for a state highway department, ran into an interesting problem implementing roundabouts to replace stop signs. Roundabouts are intersections where the automobiles don't have to stop, but instead, they go around in a circle to continue through an intersection. They typically replace stop signs at four-way intersections and are implemented to reduce the number of serious accidents when people run stop signs and crash into another vehicle. This type of accident is usually violent, causing severe injuries and deaths. Serious roundabout accidents are less likely because drivers need to slow down to maneuver through the circle.

As the department began to implement roundabouts in their state, they noticed something interesting. Although they thought the total number of accidents would decline, that didn't happen. The number of serious accidents reduced dramatically, but the number of minor accidents increased significantly. The problem was that drivers did not know how to navigate the roundabouts. This caused many minor accidents. The problem was due to a learning need. The department assumed that the public would know how to navigate through the roundabouts. The situation required the designers to put more signs in place and develop public service announcements and educational sessions for those obtaining and renewing drivers' licenses to avoid minor accidents. Learning needs are a critical part of the process.

PREFERENCES THAT NEED TO BE MET

If the individuals involved in the project don't see the value of the project, it will usually fail. Their perception is critical. Anticipating their perception, their motivation, and their acceptance of the project is vital. You may remember, or at least have heard, the story of the New Coke.[6] If not, read below.

Coca-Cola is one of the most iconic brands in the world. But in 1983, The Coca-Cola Company set out to improve quality and make a splash in the marketplace. It was then that they introduced New Coke. After spending $4 million in development and losing $30 million in back-stocked product, the product was a flop.

The failure wasn't because the public was not aware of New Coke. The recipe was tested on 200,000 people, who preferred it to the older version. New Coke failed because the market researchers needed more than a taste test. They needed to understand how people would react when the Coke they loved would be discontinued and replaced by something new and different.

Before you roll out your project, ask yourself, "How can we position this project so that those involved buy-in? How do they need to perceive this project to fully engage, learn what they need to know, and do what we want them to do?" Table 7 lists common

Table 7. Common Preferences

This solution should be:	
• Relevant to my work	• Practical
• Relevant to the community	• Easy to use
• Important to my success	• Convenient for me
• Important to the program	• New to me
• Valuable to me	• A good use of my time
• Valuable to society	• Implemented without disruption of work
• Action oriented	• Seamless with work
• Necessary given the problem	• Something that I will recommend to others
• Useful	• Something I will use

preferences among people engaged in different types of projects. Use these as a guide for planning your project rollout.

When the preferences are complete, the analysis is complete. You now have a feasible solution that aligns with the problem or opportunity you hope to address.

CONNECTING THE DOTS

Linda Green works for a nonprofit that focuses on the state prison system, particularly recidivism (the rate at which convicted felons return to prison after completing their sentence). Recidivism is a costly problem causing the state to continue to increase the size and scope of its prison system. Linda's specific area of concern is drug-related offenders. Recidivism is high—31 percent for men and 21 percent for women. In examining the prison system, Linda found very few attempts to rehabilitate prisoners with drug issues while in prison. There were no treatment and education programs structured to help them overcome their addiction. Research, case studies, and benchmarking studies have shown that these programs have worked in other prison systems, so she wanted to tackle one. She wanted to implement a treatment process mirroring other successful treatment programs. She needed to prove the value of this project to secure future funding.

Through assessing the payoff needs, Linda determined that recidivism costs the state $17,179,441 each year, just for the housing. Correcting it with an effective solution meant there would probably be a high ROI. The business need was the percent of prisoners re-arrested, convicted, and sent back to prison for drug-related crimes within three years of release from the previous incarceration.

The solution was a Drug Court Program that included treatment and education. As part of the program, inmates were to show up for their treatment and education sessions, pass routine drug testing and other monitoring assessments, and comply with court orders. To do this, the inmates would need to learn new coping skills, change their mindsets toward compliance, and change their way of thinking when it comes to the use of drugs. The inmates would also need to perceive the Drug Court Program as essential and necessary for their survival.

Table 8 presents the alignment between Linda's *How*, the Drug Court, and the state's *Why*, the recidivism of drug-related offenders.

Table 8. Aligning the How with the Why

Payoff needs	• Recidivism is an expensive problem. The cost of housing repeat offenders is $102,306,520. Of that amount, $17,179,441 is dedicated to repeat drug-related offenses.
Business needs	• Reduce recidivism rate of drug-related offenders.
Performance needs	• Because there is no treatment program, offenders continue to engage in drug-related crimes after incarceration.
Learning needs	• Offenders do not take seriously the need to change.
	• Offenders do not fully comprehend the continued consequence of their ongoing bevavior.
	• Offenders do not know of a support system that will assist them in modifying their behavior.
Preference needs	• Participants must see the Drug Court Program as important to their survival and as something they will support.

Before you implement your next project, consider what you have read so far and answer these questions:

- What is the problem you are trying to solve or the opportunity you hope to leverage?
- Is the problem or opportunity worth pursuing?
- What are the specific impact measures that need to improve?
- What performance needs to change?
- What is the most feasible solution to create the change?
- What do people need to know to do what you want them to do?
- How will you position your project so that those involved buy in?

This chapter describes the second step in the Show the Value Process: How? Select the right solution. It explains how to determine the right solution to improve the business measures identified in the first step. Sometimes, you will be addressing a problem. If so, you will need to understand the cause of the problem. Sometimes there is an opportunity, and you must determine the best way to take advantage of it. Whether a problem or opportunity, you will determine what needs to change, which will lead to the most feasible solution. When you have identified the solution, determine what people need to know to make the solution work (learning need) and how you can best roll it out so that your audience buys in (preference need).

NEXT STEPS

After completing this chapter, take these specific actions:

1. **Define your solution.** With as much detail as possible, define what you have selected to be the solution to improve the business measure. Was it an obvious solution or a not-so-obvious solution?

2. **Verify the solution.** What steps will you take to ensure your solution is the correct one? Be as specific as you can.

3. **Identify the learning needs for your solution.** This will indicate what the individuals involved in the project need to know, or know how to do, to make the project successful.

4. **Identify the preference needs for your solution.** This will indicate how you want the people involved in the project to perceive the value of the project itself.

5. **Read the next chapter.** In the next chapter, you will expect success by setting clear objectives.

CHAPTER 4

What? Expect Success with Objectives

MYTH: Objectives add little value to the outcomes.

REALITY: Objectives are powerful drivers of success.

Martin Burt, Ph.D., has a lifelong quest to understand and abolish poverty. His inspirational experience in public service includes serving as chief of staff for the president of Paraguay, the mayor of Asunción (the capital city of Paraguay), and the vice minister of commerce. Martin is the founder and CEO of Fundación Paraguaya, a nonprofit devoted to promoting social entrepreneurship and economic self-reliance to eliminate poverty worldwide.

Martin has challenged many assumptions about poverty by asking, "What if everything we knew about poverty was wrong? What if the legions of policy makers, social scientists, economists, aid workers, charities, and NGOs marching across the globe have been using the wrong strategy and tactics to wage the wrong war against poverty?"

In his book, *Who Owns Poverty?*, Martin lays out the framework necessary to eliminate poverty. The answer to his question, *"Who owns poverty?"* is clear—the people in poverty. They don't want to be in poverty. But people in poverty are not just persons with low-income labels. They are individuals with joy, generosity, and creativity. They have problem-solving and entrepreneurial spirits, and they want to rise out of poverty. They just need help and support to get there, and they will get there if we give them an avenue to do so.[1]

Martin created the Poverty Stoplight program that shows families what they must do to come out of poverty. It's not just increasing income, but it's tackling a host of issues that altogether contribute to poverty. He developed 50 indicators of poverty, as shown in Table 9. Martin created the stoplight program with clear measures and three phases: red, yellow, and green—red (a worst-case scenario), yellow (making progress), and green (out of poverty). Along with each indicator, for each phase, the Poverty Stoplight team developed specific measures of success so that all stakeholders, including the families in poverty, can see where they are going, and the progress being made. Progress follows the five-level framework of reaction, learning, application, impact, and ROI.

Table 10 provides examples of the specific definitions of some of the indicators, which let the families in poverty know when they reach the goal of yellow or green. They are positioned as objectives to define how the families should react (Level 1), what they should know (Level 2), what they should do (Level 3), the impact (Level 4), and the worth of the program (Level 5).

To make this work, Martin has trained hundreds of facilitators who are teaching and working with families to get out of poverty. The families expect success and want to have a green light status on all the indicators—that's the goal. It will take some time and support from many others to reach that goal. The program has a high probability of success. The business measures (impact) were identified in the beginning. The right solution was developed through careful research and analysis. And finally, there is a clear expectation of success with very specific objectives with key results. Through the Fundación Paraguaya and Martin's efforts, Paraguay may be the first country that becomes poverty free.

Poverty is not only a growing threat to existing institutions and the cause for much unnecessary suffering in the world but also a detriment to broad economic growth and a problem globally. Even the

Table 9. Poverty Stoplight: Indicators of Poverty

Income & Employment
Income above the poverty
  line
Stable income
Credit
Family savings
Diversified source of income
Documentation identify card
Total Category

Health & Environment
Access to drinking water
Nearby health post
Nutritious food
Personal hygiene and sexual
  health
Healthy teeth and eyesight
Vaccinations
Garbage disposal
Unpolluted environment
Insurance
Total Category

Housing & Infrastructure
Safe home
Sanitary latrine and sewer
Electricity
Refrigerator and other
  household appliances
Separate bedrooms
Elevated and ventilated cook
  stove
Comfort of the home
Regular means of transport
All-weather access roads
Fixed line or cellular telephone
Security
Sufficient and appropriate
  clothing
Total Category

Education & Culture
Know how to read, write, and
  understand Spanish
Children schooled up to 12th grade
Knowledge and skills to
  generate income
Capacity to plan and budget
Communication and social capital
School supplies and books
Access to information
  (radio & TV)
Access to entertainment
  and recreation
Values cultural traditions and
  historical heritage
Respects diversity
Awareness of human rights
Total Category

Organization & Participation
Is part of a self-help group
Impact on the public sector
Capacity to solve problems
  and conflicts
Is a registered voter and votes
  in elections
Total Category

Inferiority & Motivation
Awareness of their needs: map of life
Self-confidence (self-esteem)
Moral conscience
Emotional-affective capacity
Self-expression, beauty, and art
Violence against women
Entrepreneurship
Autonomy and decision-
  making capacity
Total Category

Source: *Who Owns Poverty?* by Martin Burt. Used with permission.

Table 10. A Sample of Poverty Stoplight Program Objectives at Each Level

After participating in the Poverty Stoplight program, participants should:

Objective	Level of Evaluation
1. Perceive the program to be relevant to their needs (4.5 out of 5).	1 (Reaction)
2. Intend to be successful with the Poverty Stoplight Program.	1 (Reaction)
3. Be able to create a plan and budget.	2 (Learning)
4. Be able to describe the three elements of a comfortable home.	2 (Learning)
5. All members of the family under 18 years of age go to school.	3 (Application)
6. At least one family member has access to formal productive credit.	3 (Application)
7. Receive vaccinations for the most serious diseases and those that are considered compulsory.	3 (Application)
8. Have a valid identity card for adult family members.	3 (Application)
9. Decrease eyesight problems by 20 percent in one year.	4 (Impact)
10. Reduce the acts of violence in their neighborhood to zero in six months.	4 (Impact)
11. Have an income above the poverty line.	4 (Impact)
12. Achieve a 20 percent ROI for the government three years after program implementation.	5 (ROI)

United States, Canada, France, Sweden, and Germany, among others, are tackling this issue.

Martin needs to show the value of the Poverty Stoplight program. He needs to push its evaluation to the ROI level for governments, as they calculate benefit-cost analysis for helping to eliminate poverty. He also needs to calculate the ROI for the companies supporting the program, showing them that this is a good investment for the company and the community. The major foundations involved in the NGOs and the charities don't need to see ROI, but they all need to see the impact. The impact is getting families out of poverty and reaching the green light on the Poverty Stoplight. Martin needs the Show the Value Process detailed in this book to show the value of what they do.

HOW TO ACHIEVE SUCCESS

You have a solution that aligns with a problem or opportunity, defined with impact measures. This chapter will help you define the *What*, meaning the expectations for success. You describe expectations in the objectives you set for a solution. Objectives represent the intended outcomes of a project. Outcomes are categorized as reaction, learning, application, impact, and ROI. Objectives are specific versus vague and nebulous outcomes. Specificity drives results. Vague and nebulous gives you, well . . . vague and nebulous. Objectives provide direction, guidance, and even motivation. They are the ultimate roadmap, and it's important to share them with all parties involved in a project, including the participants, funders, supporters, and sponsors. To best set expectations for your project's success, you will:

- Recognize the power of objectives,
- Develop specific, measurable objectives for all levels of success,
- Communicate the objectives to stakeholders that matter, and
- Use objectives as the basis for evaluating your project.

Let's dig a little deeper.

THE POWER OF OBJECTIVES

A project without objectives is like a ship without a rudder. You need something to guide you while on the journey. You need markers that tell you that you are on the right path and an indicator that tells you when you arrive at your destination. These signals also serve you as you plan your next venture.

Objectives at each level of success provide the guidance you, your team, and other stakeholders need to have a successful journey. Table 11 provides definitions and examples of objectives at each of the five levels.

Table 11. Objectives Definitions and Examples

Level	Definition	Example
Reaction	Expectations of how people involved in the project should react to and perceive the project so that you know the extent to which they buy in.	• This is relevant to my situation. • This is important to my success. • I am committed to make this work. • I would recommend this to others.
Learning	Expectations of what people must know or be able to do in order to do what you want them to do.	• Identify the four conditions for a microfinance loan. • Identify the six features of a new ethics policy. • List the five benefits of healthy living. • Demonstrate all five collaboration skills with a success rating of four out of five. • Explain the five benefits of diversity in a workgroup in five minutes.
Application	Expectations of what people should do to make the project successful.	• Within one month, participants in the youth employment program will be involved in five job interviews. • At least 50 percent of participants involved in the fitness program will join a walking or hiking group in 20 days. • Diabetic patients will implement three of the four critical behaviors in 30 days. • Participants involved in remote learning will routinely use five collaboration skills with team members each day. • Sexual harassment activity will cease within one month after the zero-tolerance policy is implemented.
Impact	Expectations of achievement in addressing the *why* of the project or the impact the project has on the key measures.	• The health status index should improve by 5 percent during the next calendar year. • Complaints of abusive force by police should reduce by 20 percent in six months. • The team should realize a 20 percent reduction in overtime in the third quarter of this year. • Unplanned absenteeism should decline by 15 percent in six months. • Process time for work visas should be reduced by 30 percent in two months.

Table 11. Objectives Definitions and Examples (*continued*)

Level	Definition	Example
ROI	Expectations of the amount returned over and beyond the investment in the project.	• Set it at the same level as capital investments in the organization. Obtain this percentage by asking the finance and accounting team for the threshold target for capital expenditures. The target is usually around 12 to 16 percent. • Set it slightly above the capital expenditure target, perhaps at 20 or 25 percent. • Consider setting it at the break-even point, 0 percent. This will indicate that you've got your money back. The break-even point is helpful because of concerns from funders. They wonder if the project benefits cover the project's cost. Remember, there are also intangible outcomes that are valuable impacts. • Let the executive, sponsor, or client set the objective. What would be their minimal acceptable performance?

Figure 2 shows what often happens with (or without) objectives. As the research over the past 60 years shows, projects without objectives may deliver some performance, but usually not much. It's questionable. You can't expect much because, after all, the people involved don't know where they are going, let alone when they'll arrive. If you have vague objectives, such as increased productivity or reduction in time, that will help, but usually not enough. First, how do you define productivity and time? How much of an increase or decrease is enough? When do you want the increase or decrease to occur? The best objectives are specific objectives. This brings in the concept of SMART requirements and what some people call objectives with key results (OKRs), as John Doerr so dramatically and vividly explores in his influential book.[2]

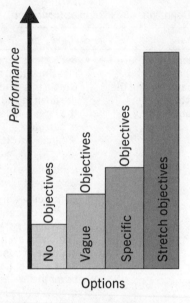

Figure 2. The Power of Objectives

If it's a team delivering the results, you need to motivate the team. One way to do that is to create stretch objectives. Objectives are the minimum acceptable performance you expect at each level from a project. Anything less, and you're disappointed. Anything more, and you're happy. However, most people like to do better than that minimum goal, and you can use the power of motivation and achievement to set a stretch objective. Let's do more. More is possible.

SPECIFICITY DRIVES RESULTS

When developing objectives, you need rules to ensure expectations are clear, easy to measure, and allow project participants to stretch their capability without feeling overwhelmed with the expectation of an impossible task. Some people refer to these as SMART objectives (Specific, Measurable, Achievable, Relevant, and Time-bound). This concept has been subscribed to for

Table 12. Rules for Objectives

1. Must be measurable and represent minimum acceptable performance.
2. Fewer objectives are better than many objectives.
3. Involve subject matter experts and key stakeholders.
4. Keep objectives relevant to the situation, program, and key stakeholders.
5. Create stretch objectives, but make sure they are achievable.
6. Allow for the flexibility to change as conditions change.
7. Failure is okay; process improvement is the key.
8. Objectives are tools for progress, not weapons for performance review.
9. Most objectives should be time-bound.
10. Provide the focus for design, development, implementation, and evaluation.

These rules are from a combination of publications:

- Jack J. Phillips and Patricia Pulliam Phillips, *Beyond Learning Objectives: Develop Measurable Objectives That Link to the Bottom Line* (Alexandria, VA: ASTD Press, 2008).
- Patricia Pulliam Phillips and Jack J. Phillips, *10 Steps to Successful Business Alignment* (Alexandria, VA: ASTD Press, 2012).
- John Doerr, *Measure What Matters: How Google, Bono, and the Gates Foundation Rock the World with OKRs* (New York: Penguin, 2018).

decades and has many variations. We use those basic concepts and add to them rules for making objectives work. Table 12 lists the rules for objectives that are practical, clear, and essential for ensuring that your objectives work for you and not against you.

To develop SMART objectives, follow these six steps:

1. Define your broad objective.
2. Identify the specific measure(s) that will tell you that you are achieving your objective. Sometimes this measure is called an indicator or metric.
3. Determine the baseline performance if you have it.
4. Set the target you hope to achieve using an estimate from one or more individuals who have expertise with the situation where the solution is implemented.
5. Include the time at which you hope to achieve the target.
6. Write your SMART objectives.

Table 13 provides an example of this process.

Table 13. Developing SMART Objectives

Broad Objective	Measures	Attributes	Baseline	Target	SMART Objective
				In three months:	Three months after the program:
Reduce time in meetings	Duration of meetings	Hours per meeting per person	2.6 hours per meeting per person	Reduce one hour per meeting per person	Time spent in meetings is reduced by one hour per meeting per person.
	Number of meetings chaired	Frequency per month	6.5 meetings per month	Reduce by two per month	Number of meetings chaired by participants is reduced by two per month.
	Number of people attending meetings	Count per meeting per month	7.2 people per meeting per month	Reduce by two per meeting per month	Number of people attending meetings is reduced by two per meeting per month.

Here is another example of how important it is to define objectives in a kind of project that normally does not have detailed objectives at the five levels. It involves a trade show exhibit at a conference in Brazil.

José Petrini is the marketing manager for a large software company in São Paulo, Brazil. His company specializes in software designed to increase the efficiency and profitability for trucking companies by helping them successfully manage their fleet, dispatch, freight, documentation, and financial operations. Part of José's responsibilities is to manage the exhibits offered by the organization at trade associations. Each year, the company exhibits at the annual conference of the Brazilian National Association of Cargo Transport and Logistics.

José manages the exhibit at the conference and follows up with individuals who visit his exhibit. Some of those leads turn into customers, but many do not. José has never thought too much about the value of this exhibit, but recently the CEO asked, "Should we continue to exhibit at the association? If so, what's the value of our exhibit?" Now José is confronting the request to show the value of what he is doing. He needs to ensure that this exhibit delivers credible value. He needs to show the ROI of the exhibit.

José is introduced to the Show the Value Process and its six steps. One of those steps is to set objectives. José has never set objectives for the exhibit before but realizes this is a good approach. He sets an objective to learn how visitors will react to the exhibit. Will the visitors find it attractive and helpful? Does it provide information that is important to them? These are reaction objectives.

José also sets objectives for learning. These are the takeaways that ask, "What do we want the visitor to learn?" He wants to make sure the visitors know about the company's capabilities, the software's reputation, and its extensive use in the trucking industry.

José also wants to make sure that he and his staff are providing visitors with specific actions to take. He wants visitors to 1) go to the website and examine satisfaction ratings from current customers, 2) view a three-minute video on the software, 3) see the list of customers who are using the software now, and then 4) to request a demonstration of their main product to manage the business. These are specific objectives for action and application.

In addition, José wants to measure the objectives for impact. He expects that current customers and new prospects will visit the exhibit. José wants to obtain at least 10 new customers and cross-sell 15 existing customers.

Finally, José decides to set an ROI objective of at least 15 percent, ensuring that the company recoups its investment plus an additional amount.

Having these very clear objectives gives everyone involved in the exhibiting process the focus they need to be successful. Success is not defined until the company actually obtains the additional upselling and new clients. This designs the exhibit to deliver success.

COMMUNICATE, COMMUNICATE, COMMUNICATE

What makes this process so powerful is that the objectives for your project are shared with everyone on the team as well as those funding the project. Objectives are the architectural blueprint for the design of your project. They tell designers what needs to happen; they tell facilitators where to take the conversation; they tell stakeholders that you've heard them and that you're on it; and they tell evaluators how to measure success.

One of the most important players in the success of your project is the manager—that significant other who can make or break any project by supporting it or standing in the way. That is why it's essential that managers receive the project objectives. In addition to setting the expectation for the manager with objectives, it is helpful to give the manager guidance on their role in the implementation of the project. In addition to the objectives, provide the managers with the following three pieces of information:

1. What they can do prior to implementation of the project to ensure its success
2. What they can do during project implementation to ensure its success
3. What they can do after project implementation to ensure its success and sustain the benefits of implementation

Table 14 describes different stakeholders in a large organization to whom you should communicate the objectives, their need for objectives, and the levels of objectives most important for them. The list is much shorter for a small organization. And in some cases, you may be the sole owner, contributor, and evaluator. The point is key players in your project need to know the objectives and their role in achieving them.

Table 14. Who Needs Objectives and Why

Role	Need for Objectives	Objectives Most Important
Performance consultant	Ensure alignment of project to business needs.	Levels 1, 2, 3, 4, 5
Designer	Create solution in a way to maximize results.	Levels 1, 2, 3, 4
Developer	Design the content of the solution to ensure proper flow and sequencing aligns with intended outcomes.	Levels 1, 2, 3, 4
Program owner	Create expectations for results. Ultimate accountability.	Levels 1, 2, 3, 4, 5
Facilitator	Explain, encourage, and validate expectations with those involved in the project. Position project for success with participants.	Levels 1, 2, 3, 4
Participant	Engage in and implement the project.	Levels 1, 2, 3, 4
Sponsor or donor	Support the program and future implementations based on results.	Levels 1, 2, 3, 4, 5
Significant other	Create expectations with team members engaged in the project as well as support implementation.	Levels 1, 2, 3, 4
Evaluator	Measure and evaluate the success of the project.	Levels 1, 2, 3, 4, 5

PLAN THE REMAINDER OF THE JOURNEY

With the objectives clearly defined, it is now time to plan the evaluation study. The planning may involve formal tools or an informal process. Including the program owner, designer, developer, performance consultant, someone familiar with the data, and possibly the client in the evaluation planning process is important. In addition to including the right people, you will:

- Clarify the purpose of the evaluation. Because you are reading this book, it is most likely that your purpose is to demonstrate the value of the project. But, as we have said in one way or another, value is different depending on perspective. So, get clear on what you mean by value and ensure that the team is clear as well.

- Ensure the feasibility of the evaluation at the different levels and confirm agreement with the targets set.
- Plan data collection by sorting out what methods you will use to collect the data, your sources for data, the timing for data collection, and who will be responsible for data collection at the time you need it.
- Plan the data analysis, including how you will isolate the effects of the project and convert impact measures to money if you did not during the first two steps of this process. Here you will also identify the costs to include in the ROI formula's denominator and potential other intangible benefits that may come from the project. You will also identify your targets for communication.

There are specific tools that can help you with your planning process. You can find them at the website. Planning your evaluation project with the team, particularly the key client, is important. It ensures everyone is on the same page—they understand what you are doing, how you are doing it, and why you are doing it that way.

ARE OBJECTIVES REALLY NECESSARY?

Some may be unmotivated to put forth the effort to set specific objectives, particularly at the impact level. Let's review what happened to Lydia Johnson when she had no objectives for her coaching program.

> The new president of Global Finance Organization (GFO), an NGO created to make loans and provide funding to developing countries, is doing what new presidents typically do: reviewing the budgets of different departments. One item caught his attention, an executive

coaching program involving 440 managers and 85 external coaches, representing a sizeable budget. This prompted a discussion with Lydia Johnson, from the talent-development area, about the value of this coaching.

The president began the conversation, "Although I'm supportive of coaching, I would like to see the ROI of this program. Do you have that?"

"No," Lydia indicated, "We have not evaluated this program at the ROI level, but perhaps we could."

The president added, "We need to do this for expenditures this large and for programs designed to help our managerial and executive teams."

With this request, Lydia Johnson needed to show the value of her coaching program with the goal of tracking the business value and the financial ROI of this program. To help with this task, GFO engaged an ROI Institute consultant. In the initial meeting with GFO, the consultant asked about the nature and scope of the program: "Are there any business objectives for this coaching program specifically detailing the business need for this coaching process?"

Lydia responds, "No, there were actually no objectives for the program, just agenda items created by the coach and some very broad goals."

The consultant continued, "When launching this program, was there a mention in the description about the business connection of the program in any way?"

"No," said Lydia.

"Was there any discussion with the participants about the business value?" asked the consultant.

Again, the answer was "no."

"Was there any correspondence or discussion with the coaches to push the coaching engagement to the business level?"

"No," replied Lydia. "The focus is on behavior. Some coaches were there for career transitions, some were there to address difficult people issues, and a few were focused on business performance."

"Good," said the consultant. "What percent focused on the business performance?"

"Well, it's really a small number," replied Lydia.

"Were there any discussions with the coaches about the specific business measures on which the managers were to focus?" inquired the consultant.

"Not really; it was left open."

The consultant summarized, "Well, there's a good chance that this program has not delivered business value—at least in terms of business measures that can be clearly converted to money, such as productivity, quality, timeliness of the projects, or specific cost savings. This may result in a negative ROI. Quite frankly, I have to ask, *"Do you really want to see the ROI for this program?"*

Lydia responded, "We have to. The new president has requested it."

The consultant replied, "The danger is that the program was not designed for the business connection, and yet we are evaluating it at the business impact and ROI levels."

"I realize this," added Lydia. "But I think our new president would be okay if we demonstrate the current value and make the changes necessary to improve its value contribution in the future."

The consultant added, "We could recommend the changes now to make it more successful. In essence, the program would begin with clear business measures in mind, and the focus throughout the coaching process would be on these business measures. We can make those changes now and moving forward to show the value of the next few groups of individuals involved in the program."

Lydia replied, "Well, we understand that, but we think we need to follow through and show the value. If it is negative, as we expect it to be, the study can include your recommendation going forward."

The consultant agreed and began the process of evaluating the program. As expected, there were no tangible measures connected to the program, although there were some very important measures, such as collaboration, teamwork, career satisfaction, and engagement. These measures were reported as intangibles because it was difficult to credibly convert them to money within this organization. As a result, it was decided not to push the evaluation to ROI but to stop with the impact expressed as intangibles. This would be used to discuss how a positive ROI could be delivered.

The good news was that the program was seen as a valuable process to participants. It was reported that the program was helpful with career issues and guiding managers through important challenges. There seemed to be some business connection, but nothing specific tied to key performance indicators. This data should provide an opportunity to improve the program going forward if the purpose of the program is to drive business. The consultant agreed to present the data to the top executives and discuss the opportunities for business value with a few changes in the process. The president reviewed the study and agreed to have a meeting to present the results to executive groups "in the near future." Meanwhile, he asked that the coaching program be placed "on pause."

Unfortunately, that meeting never occurred, and the team never had a chance to improve the coaching process. The program is still on pause.

This case study reveals that programs should start with a clear definition of success with very specific impact objectives reflecting one or more business measures. With this definition, everyone involved should expect this level of success and take steps to deliver it.

This chapter is powerful in terms of designing the project to deliver the desired results. Three things occur at this step in the Show the Value Process. First, a clear understanding and definition of the project's success are pinpointed—that's the impact. Everyone involved in the project needs to realize that success is not achieved until you have reached the impact. The second part of this step is to set clear objectives. Very specifically described objectives for reaction, learning, application, and impact provide the guidance and direction to get to where you want to go. The third step is to ensure that all the stakeholders involved have these objectives and do their part to ensure that the success is achieved at Level 4 Impact whether they develop tools, templates, and job aids, or provide support, encouragement, and assistance.

NEXT STEPS

After completing this chapter, take these specific action steps:

1. **List the reaction and learning objectives for your project.** With as much specificity as possible, indicate how you want individuals involved in the project to perceive it and what they need to learn to make it successful.
2. **List the application objectives for your project.** With as much detail as possible, list what actions, behaviors, and steps need to be taken to make the project successful.
3. **List the impact and ROI objectives for your project.** With as much specificity as possible, define the impact that will occur when the project is complete. Also include the ROI objective if you plan to take this to the ROI level.
4. **Plan your evaluation.** Think about your timing of data collection, your access to the data, the techniques you will use at different steps, and who should see the data. It is important to plan for your project before you do anything.
5. **Implement your project.** Execute the project, making it work. Be prepared to collect data.
6. **Read the next chapter.** The next chapter involves collecting the data that is detailed in this chapter.

CHAPTER 5

How Much? Collect Data along the Way

MYTH: Data collection to show the success of a project is almost impossible.

REALITY: With planning and effort, data collection becomes feasible and successful.

Suzette Haywood was the director of a major leadership-development program in a state government setting. Her team had spent more than two and a half years redesigning the leadership program into 120 hours of formal interactive training and development toward the requirements to complete an 18-month high-potential management associate program. With the redesign, the program would:

- Deliver a high-caliber developmental experience equipping associates for future leadership roles in twenty-first-century state government.
- Cultivate strong professional relationships through collaboration and team building.
- Apply experiential learning methods to work-related projects.
- Connect experienced and skilled leaders to serve as mentors and guides for current associates.

The program was the gold star emerging-leadership program for the state. It included a combination of on-the-job training, formal leadership development programming, a developmental assignment, and mentorship experiences. Upon successful completion of the program requirements, associates have the opportunity to be promoted into full-time positions within a state department.

Suzette knew that the newly designed program was powerful and important to the associates, but it was expensive, costing much more than the previous program. Although the agencies where the associates work had been paying for the program, she thought they would be reluctant to pay more for this program. Essentially, she needed to show that the program delivers more value to the agencies than the agencies were investing in it. She needed to show the value of this program at the ROI level, but she hadn't planned for this level of analysis.

Suzette collected some data about how the associates reacted to the program, what they learned in the program, and some limited data on their success using the program's leadership competencies. But Suzette needed more. She needed to know the impact of the program to develop the cost versus the benefits.

Based on comments, Suzette had anecdotal information suggesting the associates were doing amazing things in their departments, but she needed more credible data to show this. She decided to collect comprehensive data to capture more detail on how the associates were using the skill sets of the program and what impact it was having in the departments where they worked.

To validate some of the data, Suzette needed to collect data from the associates' managers to understand the impact of the efforts from their perspective. She needed detailed data on what the associates accomplished, their performance on the job, and the program's impact on the associates remaining with the state for an extended period. Each associate also completed a capstone project, and she needed the value adds of those projects.

Because Suzette had not planned for postprogram evaluation at the impact and ROI levels, she was forced to use a five-page questionnaire distributed to both the associates and their supervisors. She made every effort to obtain as much data as she could from the associates and their supervisors. To accomplish this, she needed to create interest in providing the data by explaining why it was needed, how the data would be used, and how it would recognize the associates' performance in different ways. Suzette got the top managers of the agencies involved in supporting, assisting, and providing this data. Table 15 shows 25 effective techniques to increase response. Suzette used the first 15 techniques listed.

Table 15. Techniques to Increase Response Rates

1. Provide advance communication about the questionnaire.
2. Clearly communicate the reason for the evaluation.
3. Show what's in it for them to complete it.
4. Indicate who will see the results of the questionnaire.
5. Keep the questionnaire simple and as brief as possible.
6. Keep questionnaire responses anonymous—or at least confidential.
7. Make it easy to respond.
8. Use one or two follow-up reminders.
9. Have the introduction letter signed by a top executive.
10. Have a third party collect and analyze data.
11. Communicate the time limit for submitting responses.
12. Design questionnaire with a professional format to attract attention.
13. Send a summary of results to the target audience.
14. Use the local manager to distribute the questionnaires, show support, and encourage response.
15. If appropriate, let the target audience know that they are part of a carefully selected sample.
16. Enclose a giveaway item with the questionnaire.
17. Provide an incentive (or chance of incentive) for quick response.
18. Distribute the questionnaire to a captive audience.
19. Review the questionnaire at the end of the formal session.
20. Carefully select the survey sample.
21. Allow completion of the survey during work hours.
22. Add emotional appeal.
23. Let participants know what actions will be taken with the data.
24. Provide options to respond.
25. Use a local coordinator to help distribute and collect questionnaires.

Some colleagues thought it would be impossible to get a decent response, suggesting that a 10 to 15 percent response rate would be all she could achieve. Suzette knew that would be disastrous because she was using a standard that considered missing data to be of zero value in the ROI calculation. That seemed harsh, but it was necessary to be credible. Suzette would use all the costs for the leadership program in the sample. In essence, she was using a standard to include all the direct and indirect costs and using a standard to report zero value for the missing data.

Using all 15 response rate techniques, she achieved nearly a 50 percent response rate from the associates and a similar response rate from the supervisors. The examples of the data provided were amazing. They offered great stories about their challenge projects, showing cost savings, cost avoidance, quality improvements, time savings, and many other impacts. The associates were having an impact in their departments, and it was clearly indicated in the questionnaire responses.

When the impact data was analyzed and the monetary values were provided and totaled, Suzette applied another standard to the process, omitting extreme data items. Some of the projects created substantial cost savings, and she felt the savings were too extreme. Although it was difficult to give up that value, Suzette needed to leave it out of the total benefits calculation to be very conservative.

With this conservative approach, the ROI of the program was 37 percent. When she presented the results to the senior team, they were impressed. She had data showing that the participants reacted to the program and how they perceived its value. She had data about what they had learned during the program. More importantly, she had data showing how participants used what they had learned and their success using it, along with identified barriers and enablers to success.

Additionally, Suzette had data showing the impact isolated to the program by asking the question, "What percentage of this improvement is related to this program?" Again, Suzette was following a standard to always isolate the effects of the program from other influences.

The technique she used was asking the most credible people (in this case, the participants) to provide this data. When doing so, she followed another standard in this process of using an error adjustment by asking, "How confident are you in this allocation on a scale of zero to 100 percent?" (100 percent means certainty with no error and zero meaning maximum error.) When these two numbers are multiplied, the error in the process is essentially removed.

The results were impressive, and the senior team quickly bought into the data. They were surprised because they had never seen this type of data for a soft program such as leadership development. This program was successful because it had excellent content, a design for results, and good support. Comprehensive data collection was necessary to secure the results.

DATA COLLECTION

Knowing the why, selecting the most feasible solution, and setting expectations for success are important—and are vital in designing projects that show value. But to know the progress you are making, you must collect data along the way. Data collection begins with knowing the measures to take. You can hardly create a questionnaire, for example, without questions, right? Where do questions come from? The objectives! So, the better you are at developing project objectives (reread Chapter 4), the easier it is to determine the measures you will take, how you will take them, from whom you will take them, and when you will take them. Read Zoe Moore's approach.

Zoe Moore has been very determined. She helps organizations develop their Diversity, Equity & Inclusion (DE&I) strategies by ensuring there is diverse representation in leadership and recurring professional development focused on DE&I that improves workplace culture and supplier diversity programs to increase opportunities for under-resourced businesses. She has garnished attention around the subjects, but still, many leaders ask the question, "So what? What value do diversity, equity, and inclusion bring?"

Of course, supplier diversity is important, but that is just the starting point. Equity and inclusivity are imperative across the global business of hospitality and are where the real value of Zoe's work resides. But how can she demonstrate this value? She needs to collect data about:

- How the group reacts to diversity, equity, and inclusion (reaction),
- What they are learning about the importance of DE&I and their role in making it work (learning),
- What actions they are taking and the behaviors they are changing to make this successful (application), and finally,
- What impact is occurring with the team's communication that is influencing workplace culture (impact).

This creates a new data collection stream for Zoe. While she's worked hard to improve awareness around supplier diversity through representation metrics, the challenge is to make sure that the teams integrate DE&I successfully, and she must collect data along the same five levels of success that form the value chain, with supplier diversity being the beginning point. This situation highlights that the five levels of success, first introduced in Chapter 1, can be examined at different times in projects and often from different perspectives. This requires data collection along the value chain to make it work.

A word of caution: As you design and administer your data collection approach, it will become easy for you to add one more question to the survey, one more data point from your database, one more source to your source list, or one more point in time to collect data. Don't do it. Let the process guide your journey—let the purpose and the project objectives usher you along the data collection phase. Only ask the questions you need to ask to determine whether you are achieving your objectives. Some estimates indicate that 7.5 septillion (yes, septillion) gigabytes of data are generated every day, most left unused.[1] So, why do that to your own project? Collect what you need and use it as you need. More is not better; more is merely more.[2]

To be successful with this step in the Show the Value Process, you will need to:

- Determine the method of data collection,
- Identify the sources of data,
- Minimize bias, and
- Set the timing of data collection.

Let's dig a little deeper.

DATA COLLECTION METHODS

Today it's easy to collect data. Want to know what people think about your idea? Ask them, using the polling feature in your video conferencing platform. Need to monitor success of the wellness competition? Set it up in the fitness tracker platform, and let the tracker do the work. Want to know if your team is spending too much time in meetings or is overwhelmed with too many emails? Integrate your calendar and email systems with a passive network analysis tool.

The point is data collection isn't what it once was. Yes, the fundamental techniques are the same; however, the way we administer those techniques continues to evolve making data collection easier.

Table 16 shows the typical data collection methods for four levels of data. Level 5 ROI does not require collection of data,

Table 16. Methods for Collecting Project Data at Each Level

	Level			
Method	*1* *Reaction*	*2* *Learning*	*3* *Application*	*4* *Impact*
Surveys	✓		✓	
Questionnaires	✓	✓	✓	✓
Observation		✓	✓	
Interviews	✓	✓	✓	
Focus groups	✓		✓	
Tests		✓		
Action planning/ performance contracting			✓	✓
Performance monitoring				✓

other than costs. It requires a process to convert previously collected impact measures to money and compare the monetary value to program costs.

Surveys and Questionnaires

The dominant data collection methods are surveys and questionnaires. A survey collects attitudinal measures including beliefs or opinions. Questions are usually in a yes-or-no format or an agreement-type scale. A questionnaire is more versatile, asking similar questions in addition to more in-depth questions requiring short-answer responses, rank-ordered items, and numerical data. In either case, the instruments are self-administered. This means that you send the instrument to respondents; they complete it and return it to you. Success with these instruments includes designing them for maximum convenience to the respondent and so that the responses are as objective as possible. Additionally, you want the process to be easy for respondents so that you receive as high a response rate as possible. Table 15, presented earlier, shows the techniques that are effective for obtaining a good response rate.

Observation

Observation can be powerful, particularly for Level 3 Application, data collection. When implemented correctly, it is the most accurate method of data collection because you are collecting the data in real time—watching it happen. For observation to work, the observer must be either invisible or unnoticeable. The observer must be prepared to observe and must know something about rating the behavior and recording that behavior appropriately. Observation is the only way we will know if someone is correctly performing the task. The good news is, as we mentioned earlier, that technology enables us to observe with minimal effort. The downside is that not all organizations or individuals appreciate tech-driven observation. So, if you want to use technology as your observation data collection method, become familiar with the relevant data privacy policies.

Interviews

One-on-one interviews are also powerful, but they are expensive. They provide an opportunity to probe for detail, ask the source for clarification and examples, or identify a great story. Interviews are often complementary to other data collection methods.

Focus Groups

A focus group is often more efficient than the interview. A focus group is usually comprised of 8 to 12 individuals and includes a specific agenda. The group members' data are collected confidentially, in a nonthreatening unbiased way. Group members are given equal time to provide input. This method is helpful when you want individuals in the group to hear what others in the group have to say. In essence, the other respondents are shaping the perceptions, opinions, or precision of the data. A word of caution: The operative word in focus groups is "focus." It will be easy for your focus group to go astray. So, develop a protocol, share that protocol with participants, and comply with the protocol. In doing so, you will collect useful data.

Tests

Tests can range from simple self-assessments for learning to multiple-choice, true-false questions, and even detailed problems or simulations. For many projects, the key is to have some sense that the individuals are learning what they need to make the project successful, and a simple self-assessment may be sufficient. In other situations, where having the knowledge is critical to the organization (e.g., a compliance setting) and the risk of making a wrong decision based on test results is grave and could be costly, it may be better to use a more objective testing method.

Action Planning and Performance Contracting

Another technique is to have individuals involved in the project plan what they will do with what they are learning. Action plans identify the steps they will be taking to achieve the impact. The action planning process begins with an impact measure that they want to improve and includes the action steps to achieve that impact. When the action plan has a preprogram commitment involving a significant other, it becomes a performance contract. (Inside an organization, a significant other is usually the manager of the person involved in the project. For a community-based program, a significant other would be a parent, spouse, or another individual.) Performance contracts can be powerful because you have a three-way contract for performance improvement (the person involved in the program, the person who is organizing or facilitating the program, and the significant other who is a major influencer).

Performance Monitoring

Performance monitoring means monitoring data that exists in records or databases. This method is particularly helpful for Level 4 Impact data.

Table 17 summarizes considerations for selecting the appropriate data collection method.

Table 17. Considerations for Selecting Data Collection Methods

Considerations	
Accuracy	Use the technique that will lend itself to the most accurate data, while balancing the other factors below. Some methods lead to greater accuracy than others. Observation, if implemented correctly, is the most accurate way to capture behavior and actions at Level 3 Application but can be expensive. Questionnaires, on the other hand, may not be so accurate but are inexpensive. Data in databases are assumed to be accurate and are the least expensive to collect since they already exist.
Culture	Consider the culture of the organization when selecting data collection methods. Some organizations prefer surveys and questionnaires, while others try to avoid them. Some organizations support the use of one-on-one interviews for part of the process. Others do not because they do not trust the data. In other organizations, focus groups will not work due to lack of openness, transparency, and inclusivity.
Cost	Keep costs to a minimum. Whatever you spend on data collection goes into the denominator of the ROI formula. Some methods are expensive, such as one-on-one observation or one-on-one interviews. Surveys and questionnaires are often inexpensive, which is why many organizations use them.
Disruption	Limit disruption resulting from data collection. Taking people off the job, for example, to participate in interviews and focus groups is disruptive. With observation, there is no disruption, especially if you can leverage technology. Surveys and questionnaires offer very minimal disruption, although, sending reminder after reminder to complete the survey can be annoying.
Time	Keep time required for sources to provide the data to a minimum. This will help ensure efficiency of the data collection process and will limit the distraction to your sources. Some methods, such as observation, do not require time from project participants.
Utility	Consider the usefulness of the data in making decisions. If you want to tell the story of the lived experiences of employees, you will need to interview them. If you want to predict an outcome using data, you will likely need to collect it using a questionnaire, from a database, or a combination of the two. Ask yourself, *Given the purpose of the evaluation and how I plan to use the data, will this technique provide the information I need?*

SOURCES

When collecting data, go to the most credible source(s) of data. Define credible, you say. Credible sources of data are the people or systems closest to the measures you plan to take. In many cases, the source will be the participants of the project. But there could be others, such as the participants' managers, their direct reports, customers, friends, or colleagues. Always ask yourself, *Who can answer this question most accurately?*

For example, if you want to know the productivity improvement in a specific manufacturing plant, you would not ask the senior-most executive of operations; you would go to the manager of the specific plant in question or the database the plant managers use to monitor productivity. If you want to know what the CEO thinks about the investment in learning and development programs, don't go to the chief learning officer or head of HR—go to the CEO. The point is, go to the people (or system) who own the answer to the questions you ask.

MINIMIZING BIAS

Any time people are your sources of data versus a database providing actual numerical data, some level of subjectivity and bias exists. A first step in mitigating the amount of bias in your source's response is to begin with well-developed questions.

Another approach is to communicate the purpose of your data collection and reassure potential respondents that you are not evaluating their performance. Rather, you are evaluating the project. Also, it is helpful to remind the audience that you are keeping their responses anonymous or at least confidential. By confidential, we mean that only the project team members will know who provides the data, and they commit to keeping your name separate from the data.

Additionally, as part of the questioning, you will ask respondents to identify barriers to their success. You are asking what kept them from being more successful with the project. This question provides an opportunity to push the blame for not making the project work to someone or something else. And that's exactly what they will do. They will often blame lack of success on the manager, the team, the culture, or the time needed. This is a good process to follow because it helps you obtain more complete and unbiased data for application.

Biased data is usually not a problem with impact data, because impact data are in a system. Reminding your audience of this fact is helpful, and it will reduce the likelihood of their providing arbitrary numbers. Knowing that you can fact-check the data is a good deterrent to less-than-objective responses. Also, involving their manager directly in the project will reduce their desire to exaggerate (or carelessly answer) impact data.

TIMING

Here's a quiz question for you: Where will you find the timing for data collection? The objectives! If you develop good objectives (reread Chapter 4), you will know the timing of your data collection.

Data collection for Level 1 Reaction and Level 2 Learning usually occurs during project implementation as individuals learn how to make the project successful. Learning affects reaction, so you will collect those two datasets together. It is important to collect these data during implementation to monitor participant perception of the project and ensure they know what they need to know, so they will do what you want them to do. Success with these measures is often predictive of what is to come as the project continues.

Level 3 Application data collection occurs when project participants are using what they have learned or acting as they have planned. Here you are measuring routine use of the skills, knowledge, or behaviors needed to make the project successful. Timing with these measures is a function of how complex the tasks are and the opportunity to perform them. Suppose that the project or program involves simple tasks and the opportunities for use are present every day. In that case, the participants will be using or applying the skills or information sooner than later, perhaps within a matter of days.

Timing for Level 4 Impact data collection requires that you wait until there has been time to see a consequence of knowing, information, or skill use. Application leads to a consequence or impact. Sometimes that impact occurs later than sooner. Sometimes the impact occurs immediately. So, capturing Level 4 Impact data along with Level 3 Application data may be feasible. Subject matter experts and project experts may be able to help determine when to collect impact data. Normally, Level 3 Application data are collected in three weeks to one month, and Level 4 Impact data are collected in the range of one month to six months. When exactly will it occur? In the end, it depends on the current performance of the measure, the time it will take for participants to use what they learn on a routine basis, the availability of the data, the convenience and constraints of collecting it, and when stakeholders want to see it.

DATA COLLECTION FOR LONG-TERM PROJECTS

Sometimes there are projects that require data collection at multiple times for a long period of time. Collecting data throughout the process can seem overwhelming. Renew America Together Civility Leadership Institute is one program where data are collected at multiple points in time.

General Wesley Clark (ret.) is a dedicated public servant, former four-star U.S. Army General, educator, writer, commentator, and successful businessperson. His career includes service as Supreme Allied Commander Europe, where he led NATO forces to victory in Operation Allied Force; and awards such as the Presidential Medal of Freedom and numerous honorary doctorates and civilian honors.

Because of his concern over the polarization in the United States, General Clark founded Renew America Together, designed to promote and achieve greater common ground in America by reducing partisan division and gridlock. In July 2021, Renew America Together launched a pilot program, the Civility Leadership Institute. This institute brings together business leaders, congressional staffers, city leaders, state leaders, and others who want to co-create solutions that will solve organizational and societal issues through collaboration with others whose opinions and values differ from theirs.

General Clark and Renew America Together executive director, Mary-Lee Smith, made it clear—the program must deliver impact. Because there were no specific impact measures defined, the team devised a plan to ensure the program aligned with General Clark's intent for launching the program as well as the needs of participants. Admission to the program requires applicants to provide a business case and demographic information. The business case describes their purpose for applying and the outcomes they hope to achieve. Upon selection, participants meet with the facilitator to conduct baseline assessments and learn expectations for the program.

The Civility Leadership Institute is a 12-month program with monthly learning sessions, where participants build skills in communication and influencing others. During the sessions, they also engage with some of the country's leading news makers, societal influencers, and environmental activists. Monthly sessions include ongoing collaboration and learning as well as the application of knowledge, skills, information, and insight gained throughout the program. There is a need to collect data over a 12-month period.

During each monthly session, data are collected to measure perception and intent to apply specific aspects of the content. Additionally, at the beginning of each monthly session, participants share how to use what they learn from the previous session. Data are used to adjust the programming along the way. Three months into the program, a more substantial questionnaire is administered to determine the extent to which participants are networking. Interviews between sessions allow participants to provide more in-depth feedback and share stories of how they are using what they are learning and the results they are seeing. Follow-up to the content delivery will occur via questionnaire at the 6-month and 11-month marks. The results will be delivered in month 12.

Most projects do not need such elaborate data collection. Long-term projects need multiple touch points to ensure the program is working and progress is being made. The key is to build data collection into the project, ask only the questions you need, and analyze and use the data along the way.

This chapter describes the importance of collecting data as projects are implemented. Data collection begins with the program objectives. Objectives set the expectations as described in Chapter 4. Objectives are also the foundation for the questions you will ask through the measurement process. Good objectives will inform the decisions you make regarding method, sources, and timing of data collection.

There are a variety of methods you can use to collect data. Which one (or ones) you use depends on accuracy, culture, cost, disruption, time required, and the utility that comes from the data collection method. Sources of data are always those deemed most credible. A source may include people or systems, or a combination of both. Steps should be taken to address bias of data. Timing, the final factor, depends on the time it will take for participants to use what they learn on a routine basis, and the lag between application and impact.

NEXT STEPS

After completing this chapter, take the following actions:

1. **Estimate resource requirements.** Will you be doing all the work? Will someone else be helping you? Will you

need data from others? Do you need to have meetings? What support will be needed? Do you need funding? Anticipate the resources you need along the way.

2. **List your data collection methods.** Think about reaction, learning, application, and impact—what specific methods did you use to collect each of those levels of data.

3. **Summarize all four levels of data.** Create the appropriate visuals to communicate the results, summarize the data, make conclusions, and be prepared to explain the findings.

4. **Read the next chapter.** The next chapter will cover how to analyze the data to understand the success of the project.

CHAPTER 6

What's It Worth? Analyze the Data

MYTH: The monetary value for a measure is difficult to locate or calculate.

REALITY: Most measures that matter have been converted to money.

The Kansas City SWAT team, from Chapter 2, implemented the Outward Mindset program to reduce citizen complaints about the police, a measure of the quality of their work. The team leader, Chip Huth, and the team knew they could avoid the complaints by being nice guys, but they still had their jobs to do. Measures of productivity were equally important, including confiscating drugs, cash, and guns; serving warrants; and making arrests. As a result of Outward Mindset, they were able to improve productivity and quality. Reducing complaints was an important quality measure of success. However, according to Chip, "The Outward Mindset approach did not merely help us reduce complaints, but also helped us account for an unquantifiable reduction in lawsuits, injuries, etc., and an increase in public trust, collaboration, and drug and gun seizures."

Figure 3 shows the improvement in complaints after program implementation. Complaints decreased from about three per month to zero. Chip knew that to show the value of this quality improvement credibly, he needed to account for any other factors that influenced it. The team discussed among themselves and with others, *Did anything*

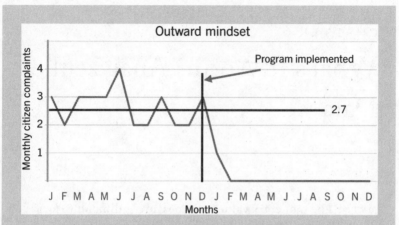

Figure 3. Isolating the Effects of the Outward Mindset Program

else cause the complaints to decrease? The number of missions did not
change, and the types of missions didn't change. There were no policy
changes and no high-profile cases in the news. In essence, the team
could not think of any other factors and believed that their new Outward
Mindset approach had made the difference. According to Chip, the complaints disappeared because of the behaviors from the Outward Mindset, "The way we responded to the reality of others while executing our
work, including some changes in procedures that were born out of
our commitment to seeing others, made the complaints disappear."

When comparing the monetary benefits of reducing complaints
for one year to the cost of preparing this team to use the Outward
Mindset, the ROI is 5,724 percent. This is an almost unbelievable ROI,
but the process and the data prove it is credible.[1]

Chapter 5 described data collection. Now comes the challenge of analyzing the data, connecting the dots, and making
sense of the results. To be successful with this step of the Show
the Value Process, you must first sort out the effects of your project from other influences. Other influences could include other
internal projects or initiatives, relevant forces, or environmental
issues. This step is vital if you want to be credible. The next issue
is converting impact data to money, which is usually easier than

it seems. Some measures are more easily converted to money than others. These are tangible data. Sometimes it's just not worth converting a measure to money, and these will remain intangible. Intangible benefits are defined as measures not converted to money because the conversion is not credible, or it takes too long to make the conversion. Then you capture the total cost of the project and compare it to the monetary benefits after the data are converted to money. This step is the ROI calculation. So, to successfully trek down this leg of the journey, you will:

- Isolate project effects,
- Convert impact measures to money,
- Determine the intangible benefits,
- Tabulate fully loaded costs, and
- Calculate the ROI.

ISOLATE PROJECT EFFECTS

When reviewing claimed improvement in business measures, the first question clients and senior executives ask is, *"How do you know it is your project that caused these results?"* The reality is that most of the time, if not always, results are due to multiple factors. So, it is important to take a step to sort the specific contribution of your project, specifically. Table 18 shows the different methods to isolate the effects of your projects. Some techniques are more research focused. Others use estimations.

Table 18. Techniques to Isolate the Effects of Projects and Programs

Research and Analytical Methods	*Estimations*
• Experimental versus control group • Trend line analysis of impact data • Use of mathematical modeling • Calculating the impact of other factors	• Participant's estimate of impact • Significant other's/supervisor's estimate of impact • Management's estimate of impact • Use of experts/previous studies • Use of customer/client input

Research and Analytical Methods

Experimental versus control group is the most credible technique. This occurs when you involve one group in a project and compare results to another similar group not in the project. The following story about a Canadian hospital shows the power of this approach.

An anesthesiologist working in a hospital in British Columbia, Canada, is a specialist in colon cancer surgery. He read about a new process developed in the UK involving a change in the preparation and after-care of patients. This new process reduced infections and readmissions, and also reduced the length of stay. He wanted to try it in his healthcare system. Funding this process would cost the system about $500,000. He knew he would be turned down, so he contacted Suzanne Schell, founder of ROI Institute Canada, to explore how to address the problem. Together they secured enough funds to try the new procedure with a small group of 16 patients. The anesthesiologist and Suzanne set out to show the new approach would save enough money to overcome the cost of implementing it beyond the pilot group.

To determine the impact of the new process, they compared the 16 patients receiving the standard preparation and aftercare. The groups were matched according to their health status, age, and other factors that could make a difference in the measures of length of stay, infections, and readmissions. They realized that they had a very small study, and it would be difficult to infer to larger numbers of patients. But they wanted to try it to make a case for a more extensive study to prove their hypothesis.

With the help of staff members, the anesthesiologist changed the procedure, trained his staff in the new procedure, and put it to work. The staff perceived it as important to the patients' health, and they willingly learned how to make appropriate adjustments in patient prep and aftercare. They followed through on those changes.

The results were dramatic. The group following the new procedure had zero complications, zero infections, and zero readmissions. Performance in the same measures for the comparison group ranged from 5 percent to 20 percent.[2]

While there are some inherent issues to consider, such as identifying and matching your groups, using control and experimental groups to isolate your project's influence on improvement in measures is widely accepted in research circles. But it is not always possible. That is why it is important to recognize other options—such as trend line analysis.

Trend line analysis begins with data in a system that are trending—either up, down, or flat. Using preproject performance, based on the trend, you then project future performance for a specific period after the project is implemented. You implement the project and track the actual performance over the time period. Then, you compare actual performance to the projected performance. The difference is the change in performance due to your project. Sounds simple, right? There are, however four conditions that must exist for this technique to work:

1. The data exist.
2. The data are stable, trending up, down, or flat.
3. There is a high likelihood that the trend would continue if you did nothing.
4. Nothing else happens during the evaluation period that would influence performance in the measure.

Chip Huth's SWAT team case study is an excellent example of trend line analysis.

Another method to isolate program's effects is mathematical modeling. This requires examining the statistical relationship between another influence and the measure being monitored. Use that relationship to forecast the improvement in the measure. In this situation, you have identified another influence that is driving your measure, and you find that there is a mathematical relationship between that other influence and your measure. If that relationship model is valid (just by asking the experts), you forecast the amount of change in your measure based on that model. If there is still improvement in the measure in question, that difference can be claimed for your project.

A simple example can help. Suppose that you have implemented a program to increase sales, and sales with existing customers have increased. You find out that during the same period, an advertising project was implemented. The marketing team has a model that shows when their advertising is implemented, the sales with existing customers increases by X amount. You find that there is nothing else happening to improve this measure, except for your project and this other influence expressed as a mathematical relationship. You use this model to forecast the increase in sales with existing customers. You notice that it's less than what the actual sales increase is in the records. You can claim the rest of that as the result of your program. This would only work if you were sure that there was nothing else happening except those influences represented by the model and your project. This would be rare, although it is gaining in popularity because of the growth of analytics in organizations. Analytics teams are often developing mathematical models showing the relationships between variables.

The last technique is similar to a pie chart that reports all the influences, including your project, and you are able to calculate with accuracy each of the other influences on the pie chart. You've accounted for all the pieces of the pie except for your project. Therefore, you can claim the amount left in the pie as your improvement. This would be applicable only if the other factors are identified and if you can easily and credibly calculate the impact of those factors. This would be extremely rare, but it could be a remote possibility. It's worth at least giving it some consideration.

Using Estimates

When research and analytical methods don't work, let your most credible sources help you sort it out. Sometimes these will be the individuals involved in the project, and sometimes they will be their managers or others. To do this, follow these steps:

- Start with the improvement in the measure, which is a fact.
- Ask your most credible source three questions:
    1. What caused the improvement?

2. As a percentage, how much of the improvement is due to the project?
3. How confident are you in your estimate?

The result of this process is a conservative estimate based on what your sources believe to be true. While not our preferred approach, this is a good fallback method when the other techniques are not feasible. In fact, we've validated the conservative nature of this process by comparing the amount with that of experimental design. As expected, the estimates are less than the differences in the two groups after the adjustment for error. Estimates represent essentially the wisdom of the crowds, which is a popular and powerful approach to collecting data.[3] For more information on this topic, see other resources.[4]

CONVERT DATA TO MONEY

After you isolate the impact of your project from other influences, the next step is to convert the impact to monetary value. There is good news: there's a good chance that the measure(s) of interest already have a monetary value. You just need to find it. Table 19 presents the methods of converting data to money, and they often involve simply finding the value already calculated.

Table 19. Methods of Converting Data to Monetary Values

- Converting output to contribution—standard value (profit/savings)
- Converting the cost of quality—standard value
- Converting employee's time (using compensation)
- Using historical costs/savings
- Using internal and external experts
- Using data from external databases/studies
- Linking with other measures
- Using participants' estimates
- Using supervisors' and managers' estimates
- Using staff estimates

Standard Values

A standard value is one that has already been calculated, reported, and accepted by executives. For example, in Chip Huth's case study (presented in Chapter 2 and again in this chapter), the police department had already calculated the cost of investigating a citizen complaint. It was the "standard." Communicating this value to the team let them know the magnitude of the problem. Most organizations have standard values for measures of productivity and quality measures.

Time savings also have a standard value—the hourly rate (fully burdened) of the person's time. If your project saves someone four hours a week, that's worth four hours of pay plus benefits. A word of caution: time savings are a benefit of your project only if the person(s) uses their time savings on other productive work. This means you must clarify time savings. You can do this by asking the simple question, "What percentage of the time saved was used on productive work?" and requesting examples of the other productive work.

Internal and External Experts

If there is no standard value, then look for known experts. Internally, they will be the individuals who deal with the measure. They track and monitor it routinely. They address it, work with it, and report it. If it's a quality measure, then it's the quality team. If it is a safety measure, then it's the safety team.

If experts do not exist within the organization, there may be external experts. You may find names of external experts in databases, books, and articles, and from colleagues.

Databases and Studies

The good news is the internet has an ample amount of data. You can find values for productivity, quality, work habits, employee satisfaction, and even happiness. The key is to vet your research. Where does it come from? Who conducted the study and why? Are there multiple independent studies pointing to the same result? Is it credible enough for your audience? Also, consider time to research. It is easy to venture off the beaten path when perusing for monetary values. An easy approach—ask-a-librarian. You simply describe to them what you want, and they send it to you—citations and all.

Darnell Jackson serves on the police force of a college town. The city has grown as the university has grown, creating some of the usual issues of a larger city, such as traffic, congestion, and crime. Motor vehicle thefts have recently increased well above the average for cities the size of Darnell's, and they are above the national average on a per capita basis.

This problem is worth solving because motor vehicle theft is not just an inconvenience for the victims of the crime, but there are other costs for them, the insurance companies, and the judicial system. Darnell knows that the police chief has many priorities, and motor vehicle theft might not be the biggest concern. But the payoff for solving the problem could be huge. Darnell decides to tackle the project for the community.

Through his investigation, Darnell realizes many motor vehicle thefts could have been prevented. Most occur because students leave their cars unlocked and, in some cases, leave their keys inside. Darnell wants to develop resources to educate the community. He believes the situation will improve by focusing on the vehicles most likely to be stolen and with more awareness of the issues. His project will cost time and money, but Darnell thinks it will be worth it. He wants to show the ROI of the project to the chief.

In order to get started, Darnell needed to lock down the cost of a motor vehicle theft, but he didn't have the time to calculate it, and he didn't necessarily have anyone on the team who could do it. So, he looked online, and he found the Rand Corporation website. He found a webpage from the Center on Quality Policing, and a report, "Hidden in Plain Sight: What Cost-of-Crime Research Can Tell Us About Investing in Police."[5]

From Darnell's perspective, the website was perfect because Rand had no real agenda when developing and reporting the research.

Rand Corporation is a nonprofit organization without any sponsors. There was no reason why they would want this number to be high or low, and they were transparent with their calculations. More importantly, Darnell saw that other police functions use this data—confirmation that it was credible enough for him to use.

It turned out that the cost for one motor vehicle theft was $9,079, and the city had reported 648 thefts within the last year. This yielded a total cost to the city of $5,883,192, making the magnitude of the problem even more evident to Darnell and to the chief.

Darnell then moved forward to validate that his solution to reducing motor vehicle thefts was worth the investment. He set the project objectives, designed his solution with those objectives in mind, and evaluated its success.

By leveraging the work of Rand Corporation, Darnell converted motor vehicle theft to money, made a compelling business case to solve the problem with his solution, and used the value to evaluate the success of his project.

If you need to convert a measure to money and do not have standard values or experts to help, "search" for it.

Linking with Other Measures

There are two possibilities with this method. One is to try to link a measure that's hard to value, such as employee engagement to a measure that's easier to value, such as revenue per employee or retention. Analytics teams in some organizations do this type of analysis routinely. Maybe yours is one of them.

Another approach is to calculate the cost of a particular measure. For example, you want to calculate the cost of a customer complaint, review many customer complaints, and track the impact of one on the organization. Determine the value of each complaint (considering its impact), and take the average value of the complaint. This method is useful when the conversion has not yet been done, but it takes a lot of time.

Estimates

Apart from the experts, the analysis that could be done, and finding the value already calculated, it might be good to get others to provide the estimate. These could be the individuals involved in the project, their managers, or others who may have input. Again, the estimates must be credible and then adjusted for error as described earlier. This is important, and this is doable.

DETERMINE THE INTANGIBLES

When an impact measure cannot easily be converted to money credibly within a reasonable amount of time, then it remains an intangible. This doesn't diminish the importance of the measure. It just means that it's not credible to convert it to money, or it takes too long to convert it to money. The world is full of intangibles, and reporting how your project influences them can be powerful. Table 20 shows you the broad scope of typical intangibles in an organization.

The key is to make sure to connect the intangible to the project. You can do this by using the isolation techniques previously mentioned or by simply asking the individuals involved in the project to tell you the extent to which this project has influenced this measure, usually on a 1- to 5-point scale. While not ideal, this technique does provide an indication that the project contributes to the important intangible measures.

WHY EMPLOYEE ENGAGEMENT USUALLY REMAINS AN INTANGIBLE

We have made progress credibly converting many of the softer measures to money. One measure that we typically do not convert is employee engagement. Employee engagement is essentially a satisfaction measure that has evolved as management research has evolved. How you measure employee engagement

Table 20. Common Intangibles

• Agility	• Happiness
• Ambiguity	• Human life
• Alliances	• Image
• Awards	• Intellectual capital
• Brand	• Job satisfaction
• Burnout	• Leadership effectiveness
• Capability	• Loyalty
• Capacity	• Mindfulness
• Carbon emissions	• Mindset
• Clarity	• Net promoter score
• Collaboration	• Networking
• Communication	• Organizational commitment
• Compassion	• Partnering
• Complexity	• Patient satisfaction
• Compliance	• Poverty
• Conflict	• Reputation
• Corporate social responsibility	• Risk
• Creativity	• Social capital
• Culture	• Stress
• Customer service	• Sustainability
• Decisiveness	• Team effectiveness
• Emotional intelligence	• Timeliness
• Employee attitudes	• Trust
• Engagement	• Uncertainty
• Food security	• Volatility
• Grit	• Work/life balance

depends on how you define the construct, what measures provide you the information you need, and how much you are willing to spend.

Engagement is a powerful measure. It can tell you how emotionally connected employees feel to the organization and about their desire to contribute to organization excellence. Engagement can be a strong predictor of employee retention, safety incidents, productivity, and other impact measures.

There are four reasons employee engagement remains an intangible rather than a monetary benefit for a project. First, executives sometimes fund projects based on their intuition that if engagement is high, good things will happen. If disengagement is high, bad things will happen. Visions of employee disengagement include low productivity, mistakes, sloppiness, and departures, along with dissatisfaction. So, executives often fund projects that lead to engagement to prevent disengagement.

Second, studies show significant relationships between measures of engagement and the all-important operational and strategic measures, such as productivity, retention, and customer satisfaction. Showing the power of engagement from these macro-level studies may be enough for some executives.

Third, while soft, in that it is based on subjective responses, it is a construct that has been defined and validated, even though the measures may be different. For example, Gallup and Utrecht went to great lengths to ensure their measures of employee engagement were valid.[6] Each, however, measures engagement differently. The point is that engagement is measurable and meaningful. Therefore, executives recognize the value of the measure and of improving the measure when performance is lacking.

Finally, engagement as an intangible is powerful, and there has been little pressure to determine the monetary value of improving it. This means there have not been many ROI studies on employee engagement efforts, although there are some. We wrote a book on this process with case studies showing it can be done.[7] But, most executives seem to be comfortable leaving engagement as an intangible measure when they are sure its improvement is connected to the project.

TABULATE FULLY LOADED COSTS

Investments in projects go far beyond what you pay for a contractor, or your time developing and delivering it. The cost of the project should include all the costs, direct and indirect. Table 21 shows a complete listing of project costs. It is important for your project that you make sure you examine every cost. Some costs will be there because you had to pay for them, or you were charged for them. Others are included because you took

Table 21. Project Cost Categories

Cost Item
Initial analysis and assessment
Development of solutions
Acquisition of solutions
Implementation and application
Salaries/benefits for project team time
Salaries/benefits for coordination time
Salaries/benefits for participant time (if appropriate)
Project materials
Hardware/software
Travel/lodging/meals
Use of facilities
Capital expenditures
Maintenance and monitoring
Administrative support and overhead
Evaluation and reporting

some individuals away from their work, losing their productivity, so you include the salaries and benefits for that time. To keep this simple, review every step in your project, from the design, development, implementation, evaluation, and reporting. All the costs must be included to make the ROI calculation credible. Estimates of the indirect cost will suffice.

Gloria Williams was asked to help reduce the turnover of communications specialists in a large security agency. Because of the technology they employed, this agency attracted new college graduates to join the team. Unfortunately, after a year or so of experience, team members could double or triple their salaries if they joined a private-sector firm, something Gloria's organization could not match due to caps on salaries based on time, grade, and degree.

Exit interview data suggested that most of the turnover was due to salary. However, turnover dropped significantly if team members stayed five years or longer. At the same time, the agency was always employing the latest technology, most of which was unavailable in other organizations. This made continuous investment in upskilling essential for the 1,500 specialists. In addition to training on the new technology, some team members expressed interest in earning a master's degree in information science.

With the help of a local university, Gloria explored the opportunity of offering a master's degree in information science inside the agency, on agency time at no charge to the employees. This offering would be a lucrative benefit to team members and the agency. To make it work, Gloria needed to show that the program delivered more value than it cost.

Her impact measures were reduction in turnover and increased capability with the new technology through the upskilling program. Based on focus groups and exit interview data, she felt confident the solution would work. Given that the master's degree was offered with a service contract of two additional years after they completed the degree, the fact that team members expressed interest in earning the graduate degree, and program content would deliver the technical capability the agency required, Gloria felt the program would be a solid win. She decided to pilot it with 100 specialists.

To conduct an ROI study showing the value of this program, Gloria needed to research the costs. She knew they would be significant. The agency was paying a premium amount for the tuition because the professors had to travel to their agency. The professors were not only traveling but also were securing a top-secret security clearance.

Gloria had to make some decisions. Should she include every cost? She concluded she had to meet the criteria of the Show the Value Process. That meant accounting for the participants' time away from work. Although many of the participants might make up the time to keep current with their work or have someone else fill in and do it for them, still, they were absent for at least an hour at a time, and Gloria knew she had to account for a lot of time over the three-year period that it would take to complete the master's degree. Gloria included all the costs, which are shown in Table 22.

Table 22. Total Fully Loaded Costs of Master's Program for 100 Participants

	Year 1	Year 2	Year 3	Total
Initial analysis (prorated)	$1,667	$1,667	$1,666	$5,000
Development (prorated)	3,333	3,333	3,334	10,000
Tuition—regular	300,000	342,000	273,000	915,000
Tuition—premium	50,000	57,000	45,500	152,500
Salaries/benefits (participants)	899,697	888,900	708,426	2,497,023
Salaries/benefits (program administrator)	53,650	55,796	58,028	167,474
Program coordination	15,000	15,000	15,000	45,000
Facilities	43,200	43,200	34,560	120,960
Management time	3,000	3,000	3,000	9,000
Evaluation	3,333	3,333	3,334	10,000
Total	$1,372,880	$1,413,229	$1,145,848	$3,931,957

Gloria's case study describes the importance of including all the costs of the program.[8] The benefits were greater than the cost of the program. The benefits were $8,365,000 for turnover and $1,580,000 for capability. When these benefits were combined and compared to the costs, a very credible ROI of 153 percent was delivered. Ultimately, the program was considered a success.

CALCULATE THE ROI

At this point, you know the monetary benefits of the project, which we call project benefits, and you know the project costs. Now, calculate the ROI using the two most common measures for ROI. The first calculation is the benefit-cost ratio (BCR).

The BCR has its origins in the public sector where centuries ago governments were conducting cost-benefit analysis. The BCR is still an important measure in government, nonprofits, and nongovernmental organizations.

The second calculation is the ROI calculation, which comes from the finance and accounting field. Its earliest use was by the Dutch East India Company, founded in 1602, as it was the first company to offer equity shares of its business to the public. Other measures of return on investment have evolved, but the most fundament calculation is the net monetary benefits minus the costs divided by costs times 100, allowing us to use a percent. Table 23 shows the actual calculations of these two critical measures.

A benefit-cost ratio, as in this example, of 2.18 means that for every dollar you invest, you have $2.18 in benefits. With ROI, the 118 percent means that for every dollar you invest,

Table 23. The Benefit-Cost Ratio and Return on Investment Calculations

Defining the Benefit-Cost Ratio

$$\text{Benefit cost ratio (BCR)} = \frac{\text{Project benefits}}{\text{Project costs}}$$

Example
Project benefits = $71,760
Project costs = $32,984

$$\text{BCR} = \frac{\$71,760}{\$32,984} = 2.18$$

Defining the Return on Investment

$$\text{ROI (\%)} = \frac{\text{Project benefits} - \text{Project costs}}{\text{Project costs}} \times 100$$

Example
Project benefits − Project costs = $71,760 − $32,984
Project costs = $32,984

$$\text{ROI (\%)} = \frac{\$71,760 - \$32,984}{\$32,984} \times 100 = 118\%$$

you earn the dollar back plus another $1.18. These calculations are two ways of showing the same thing. We suggest that you calculate both to show your audience that these two measures, which are so common, are really the same data sets. This also meets your audiences' needs because some individuals prefer BCR, and others prefer ROI.

THE RULES TO FOLLOW

Whether you use the BCR, ROI, or both, to ensure you tell the best story with the most reliable data, you need to follow a set of rules—or what we call, guiding principles. Table 24 summarizes the rules of the road and their meaning.

So, there you have it—the steps you take when analyzing data. Showing the impact and ROI of what you do, which is the basis for this chapter, is powerful and necessary for some projects. And doing so credibly requires you to first isolate the effects of your project, convert at least some measures to money,

Table 24. Rules of the Road

Rule	Its Meaning
1. Tell the complete story of success.	When conducting a higher level of evaluation, collect data at lower levels.
2. Use the most credible sources.	When collecting and analyzing data, use only the most credible sources.
3. Choose the most conservative alternative.	When analyzing data, select the most conservative alternative for calculations.
4. Give credit where credit is due.	Use at least one method to isolate the effects of the solution.
5. Make no assumptions for nonrespondents.	If no improvement data are available for a population or from a specific source, assume that no improvement has occurred.
6. Adjust estimates for error.	Adjust estimates of improvement for the potential error in the estimates.
7. Omit the extremes.	Extreme data items and unsupported claims should not be used in ROI calculations.
8. Account for all project costs.	Fully load costs of the solution when analyzing ROI.

and account for the full costs of your project. The next question is, however, "*So what?*" Now that you have the results, how do you communicate them to get what you want when you began the journey? How can you use the data to improve your project or the processes that support it in the future? Chapter 7 answers the so-what question.

NEXT STEPS

After completing this chapter, take these next steps:

1. **Identify your method of isolating the effects of this program on the impact data.** Taking this step will ensure credibility of your results.
2. **Identify your method for converting data to money.** Also, indicate how you calculated total monetary benefits of the project. This step is necessary to describe the magnitude of the impact and compare it to the cost when calculating ROI.
3. **Capture the total project costs.** To be credible, include all the direct and indirect costs.
4. **Highlight the intangible benefits.** To be credible, show how the intangible measures directly relate to the project.
5. **Calculate the benefit-cost ratio and the ROI.** Be prepared to explain both calculations.
6. **Read the next chapter.** Chapter 7 focuses on leveraging the results.

So What? Leverage the Results

MYTH: The success of one project rarely influences investing in another project.

REALITY: The best results to continue to invest in are previous successes.

Jessica Kriegel, an organization and talent development consultant at Oracle with expertise in strategic planning, talent management, and leadership development, was particularly focused on intergenerational understanding. More specifically, she realized that generational labels do not work. The labels aren't bad. It's the associations that society puts on those labels that are bad.

Although labels abound with each generational era, millennials (those born between 1980 and 2000) are the most misunderstood generation. These labels keep individuals, managers, and even organizations from being as successful as they should be. Jessica's work at Oracle provided her with an opportunity to tackle this challenge directly. One project clearly focused on this challenge, and she needed to show its value.[1]

A product-development team member reached out to the person in charge of the Oracle College Hire Program about their problem with the millennials. The team member suggested that the millennials didn't understand the corporate culture, and as a result, there were behavioral and communication issues. This suggestion included a request for a training program to help the millennials acclimate to the company.

Jessica took this project on. She wanted to understand the issue and ensure that the correct program was implemented. She did not want to take on the project on the face value that millennials were the problem, and if we fix them, everything is okay.

Each year, this program develops approximately 100 to 200 new college hires, making this an important program. She examined some of the data that were surrounding the situation. A lack of productivity was reported, along with the excessive turnover of the millennials. Some were leaving soon after employment, which was very expensive. Consequently, the business outcomes of interest were improved productivity and reduced turnover.

To understand the right solution, Jessica conducted a detailed survey with the managers and the employees. The surveys indicated that:

- New hires sometimes struggle with acclimating to the company,
- There was almost no intergenerational conflict,
- A few differences were perceived across generations, and
- Both the new college hires and the managers seemed to enjoy their work and working together.

Next, Jessica conducted focus groups to examine the problem in more detail, and the focus groups identified areas where improvement was needed. The managers:

- Felt that the generational cohorts were different,
- Claimed that the millennials did not understand the difference between social and professional networking, and
- Thought that millennials had low emotional intelligence.

Meanwhile, the millennials felt they:

- Needed more information about why their jobs mattered,
- Wanted more communication from their manager, and
- Were struggling to find a work-life balance.

With these issues identified, the solution was designed to work with both groups to ensure that they worked productively and efficiently together, addressing their individual needs in two different programs (one for the managers and one for the employees). She set out to show the value of her program.

As Jessica conducted the programs, she captured reaction data. The employees felt the program was valuable, and it helped them understand more about their roles in the organization. She measured learning from both groups and found they were learning what they needed to do to be more successful. She measured application to see the extent to which they were working together because of the training. The reports were positive that they were working collaboratively. With the increased collaboration came improvements in retention and productivity. With these improvements, she took a step to sort out the effects of the program from other influences, converted these measures to money, compared program benefits to the cost of the program, and calculated that the return on investment was 695 percent. The executives were impressed, and she communicated the results to other groups and included a copy of her bestselling book, *Unfairly Labeled*.

Leveraging the results of Jessica's project has made a difference—not only for the organization in which she was working at the time, but also for the program participants and the individuals she now reaches through her writing and speaking.

The point of this chapter is "So what? Leverage the Results." You may have a sound theory on which to base your project. You may have done a remarkable job aligning your project to the needs of the business, implementing the project, and even evaluating the project. But until you act on the information that comes from the data gathered, you have done nothing but, well, executed another activity. Evaluation without action is useless. To complete the final leg of the Show the Value journey, you will:

- Communicate results,
- Optimize results, and
- Leverage results.

COMMUNICATE RESULTS

Communicating results as you collect and analyze data is the hallmark of good evaluation. Why go to all the trouble if you're not going to share, right? When it comes time to tell the final story of your journey, you will be armed with six types of data (reaction, learning, application, impact, ROI, and intangibles). Your presentation will tell the story of how participants reacted to the project, what they learned to make the project work, what steps they took to make the project successful, and the barriers and enablers to their success. The story will describe the impact of the project and the financial return on investment of the project. In addition, you will report the other intangible benefits of the project. The key is to present the right data to the right audiences.

Table 25 shows some common target audiences, particularly for larger projects in larger organizations. The list gets much shorter if you are in a small group or working on a smaller project. As you consider your audience, consider the purpose of your presentation—how you want audience members to react, what you want them to learn, what you want them to do, and the impact you hope to achieve by presenting results. Think about the "why" for communicating results and align your presentation with the why. Set specific objectives to ensure your that communication achieves the results you want. In essence, you will design your communication to deliver value!

Next, select the best methods of presenting the information to your audience. Table 26 shows a variety of methods for communicating results. Just one or two methods may be appropriate for a small project involving a small group. A more extensive project involving a larger group in a larger organization may require several methods to deliver the information to those who

Table 25. Common Target Audiences

Primary Target Audience	Reason for Communication
Client	• To secure approval for the project
Managers	• To gain support for the project
Participants	• To secure agreement with the issues
Top executives	• To enhance the credibility of the project leader
	• To improve the results and quality of future feedback
Immediate managers	• To reinforce the processes used in the project
	• To prepare participants for the project
Project team	• To drive action for improvement
	• To create the desire for a participant to be involved
Key stakeholders	• To show the complete results of the project
Support staff	• To explain the techniques used to measure results
All employees	• To demonstrate accountability for expenditures
Prospective participants	• To market future projects

Table 26. Methods of Communication

• **Meetings**	• **Brief Reports**	• **Mass Publications**
○ Executives	○ Executive summary	○ Announcements
○ Management	○ Slide overview	○ Bulletins
○ Stakeholders	○ One-page summary	○ Newsletters
○ Staff	○ Brochure	○ Brief articles
• **Detailed Reports**	• **Electronic Reporting**	○ Press releases
○ Impact study	○ Website	
○ Case study (internal)	○ Email	
○ Case study (external)	○ Blog / social media	
○ Major articles	○ Video	

need it. For each method and each audience, develop the content to support their needs, making sure they have the right amount of information at the right time to act.

When working with your sponsors, the individuals who want to see the data and care most about the outcome, it's helpful to conduct a briefing. This is a critical meeting where the project's success is in play. Your sponsors will also evaluate the process you use to capture the data and analyze results. Its acceptance is vital. Table 27 shows the sequence of a typical project evaluation

Table 27. Presentation Sequence

---

1. Describe the project and explain why it is being evaluated.
2. Present the evaluation process.
3. Present the reaction and learning data.
4. Present the application data.
5. List the barriers and enablers to success.
6. Present the business impact (with isolation and conversion to money).
7. Show the costs.
8. Present the ROI.
9. Show the intangibles.
10. Review the credibility of the data.
11. Summarize the conclusions.
12. Present the recommendations.

---

briefing with a sponsor or group of executives. Carefully plan your briefing because much is at stake. You may be presenting to skeptical executives who want to make sure that everything is credible, so that they can support the process. If they can support your process, they will support the results. If they don't support your process, they won't support your results—so, the two go together. There are many detailed examples of this process available.[2]

In the last chapter, we introduced an anesthesiologist working at a hospital in British Columbia, Canada, and Suzanne Schell of ROI Institute Canada. The anesthesiologist is part of a colon cancer surgery team. A new process, developed in the UK, had been reviewed by the team. This new approach involved a change in the preparation and aftercare of patients. The new process reduced infections, readmissions, and length of stay.

The anesthesiologist and Suzanne were able to determine the cost of avoiding complications, infections, and readmissions. The total of these avoided costs was significant. Next, they spoke with finance and accounting to determine the monetary value for reducing length of stay. They had a value that they thought they could defend, but it was a value that could be debated. Some people could say that because they were a government-funded healthcare system, when the length of stay is reduced for one patient, another patient will simply come in and occupy the bed. Therefore, it doesn't necessarily save the hospital money. Although this is very narrow thinking, there is some monetary value associated with reducing the length of stay. Suzanne and the anesthesiologist didn't want to have this presentation turn into a debate on the value of the length of stay, so they left the measure as an intangible.

The presentation strategy was to show the stakeholders the power of the new process and make a case for a larger study, recognizing that a sample size of 16 is not enough to make a major decision. Suzanne and the anesthesiologist were surprised at how the stakeholders reacted to this new approach; they saw that it produced dramatic results and that it represented an ROI of 118 percent. Suzanne and the anesthesiologist received support to change the procedure, even without a larger sample size. Even the chief financial officer of this healthcare unit said that he could clearly see cost savings with this new process and that it would pay for itself quickly.

The new procedure is now in place. Based on the success that it was experiencing, other provincial health systems in Canada began to adopt the new procedure, and now the new process has been implemented throughout the Canadian healthcare system. This came about because one anesthesiologist, with the help of a consultant, wanted to show the value of what he believed would be a change in the process worthy of pursuing.[3]

Sometimes it's important to not only measure the success of one project but also a group of projects or all the projects under the responsibility of an individual. Here's a story where a scorecard was developed showing the value of all the events that Mi Cha Yoo is evaluating.

Mi Cha Yoo is a manager of events for a large Korean automobile company. She recently became concerned that the value of her function has come into question. She has been asked several questions about contribution, value, and measurement of the function, and she is concerned that without clear data showing the value of the function, her work could be marginalized in the future. Previously, Mi Cha had collected data about the success of each event, detailing how individuals have responded to those events—but this has been the only information available, and she needs more to validate her work. Mi Cha uses the model in this book as a framework to show the value. She not only collects reaction data about each event in terms of relevance and necessity but also measures the takeaways—the actual learning—from each event. She then combines this into a scorecard to provide a clear profile of important reaction and learning data.

Next, she follows up on a significant number of events to understand what individuals have used from what they learned—the actions from their takeaways. Using consistent questions, she compiles these successes as important measures of action from each event. Finally, for a select number of events, she measures the impact the events have had on sales, delivery, service, and cost control. Although these data are compiled by individual projects, she combines the results to create an overall scorecard of performance. She is now able to show not only the reaction to the experience, but the reaction to the content of the events, the takeaways (learning), the specific actions taken, and the impact on the organization.

For at least a couple of events each year, Mi Cha calculates the financial ROI by showing the cost of the event compared to the monetary benefits when the impact data are converted to money. This has enabled Mi Cha to show the value of her function in ways the executives have not seen before. It has increased her influence, respect, and her funding.

OPTIMIZE RESULTS

Your work is not done after you communicate results. You must use the results to influence key decision makers and drive change in the project and the system that supports project implementation. Evaluation is not just about demonstrating value—it's also about creating even greater value through process improvement.

Process Improvement

Although there are many reasons to evaluate a project, one of the most important reasons is to make the project better. That's the heart of the Show the Value Process—improvement using black box thinking. Figure 4 illustrates that process. Black box thinking comes from the aviation industry, where black boxes are retrieved after an airplane crashes. The voice data recorder and the systems recorder are examined to see what caused the accident. When the cause is known, decisions can be made about what changes are necessary to prevent similar accidents from happening. This process occurs by regulation and law, and consequently, this has made aviation the safest way to travel.

Bring that same thinking to your project. If it's successful, make it more successful. If it fails to deliver, improve it. Measurement leads to evaluation, and improvement leads to optimization. By optimizing the results, you increase the value by adjusting the current project, the next offering of the project, or the next project. When you do this, you can influence project funding and position funding allocation opportunities in your favor. This approach will help you attain the budget to improve the next project or implement the same project in other places.

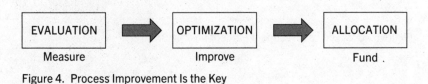

Figure 4. Process Improvement Is the Key

Cost versus Investment

Calculating ROI using a standard formula from the finance and accounting field is the way to prove to executives that your project is an investment, yielding a positive return. Your presentation of results convinces executives that what you are doing is an investment, not a cost. Contrast that with so many other projects and programs in which executives consider only costs because they haven't seen the positive ROI value. When this value is presented, you experience the reality explained in Figure 5, costs versus investment.

If your project is considered a cost, there will be efforts to control it, freeze it, pause it, reduce it, or eliminate it. Consequently, partnerships are rare, influence diminishes, support is lost, and future funding, of course, is curtailed. But if the project is considered an investment, the opposite can occur. Executives may maintain the investment, allocate more resources to it, and protect it. Partnerships can develop because all parties can see the value of what you do. Relationships with clients improve because they understand the value you deliver. Ultimately, you will have that previously elusive seat at the table.

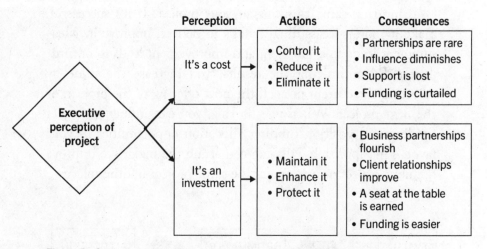

Figure 5. Cost versus Investment Perception: The Reality

LEVERAGE RESULTS

It's important to use your results to the maximum advantage, much as Jessica did in the beginning story. Yes, you will use results to improve a project and the processes surrounding it. But to leverage the results means that you will exploit the results to create even greater awareness, change, and value. Here are several examples of what we mean by leveraging results, in addition to Jessica's story.

Return to Chip's Story

Chip Huth's story, presented in Chapters 2 and 6, continues. The fantastic results of reducing citizens' complaints to zero resonated quite well with the leaders and others. During that same period, the Kansas City SWAT team received awards for the productivity they delivered. Not only did they improve quality by reducing complaints, but they also improved productivity. Chip began to make presentations to groups and even presented a TEDx Talk with literally hundreds of thousands of viewers. Now he works part time with the Arbinger Institute to help spread the word about the Outward Mindset product line. Additionally, Chip was promoted to the rank of major and now serves as a division commander of the Kansas City Police Department. He has done an excellent job of leveraging the results of this project.

Tackling a New Approach

Juan Pablo, a marketing analyst for Bimbo Bakery, Barcelona, Spain, was interested in using social media advertising for the firm. To date, Bimbo had not been involved in social media advertising but wanted to pursue, or at least explore, this concept. To use it properly, Juan decided to attend the annual conference of the American Marketing Association (AMA), including a preconference workshop on using social media advertising. At the conference, Juan planned to attend several sessions related to the use of social media with topics about effectiveness, processes, pitfalls, and best practices.

Juan attended the conference with a clear focus and used the Show the Value Process to evaluate this effort. He only attended sessions concerning topics that were relevant to his project, important to his own success, and had a practical aspect (the reaction). Juan paid close attention to sessions, collecting information about ways to buy media advertising, ad design principles, implementation tips, specific measures of effectiveness, and so on (learning). Immediately upon his return, Juan explored the possibilities, followed up on some of the marketing contacts, studied the case studies, contacted social media ad agencies, and ultimately initiated a project (application). With Juan's project in place, using what he had learned from the conference, he measured the impact of the ads and contrasted the effectiveness of the advertising with traditional advertising (impact).

Next, considering the cost and benefits, Juan compared the approach of the new media, including the cost of his time, travel, and fees for the AMA conference. This yielded a positive ROI on his venture, clearly showing the organization that this new process had a value-add.

Your Sponsors May Ask for More

Kaycee Buckley is a global senior training manager for a major healthcare organization. Recently, she was concerned about the value of a coaching program she had organized. It seemed that the sales managers might not be coaching the sales team the way they should, but Kaycee wasn't sure. So, she decided to evaluate the value of the coaching process to determine how it was working and how it connected to actual sales.

Kaycee completed her evaluation following the process presented in this book only to find out—just as she suspected—that the managers were not coaching very well or at all in some cases. This lack of action resulted in a negative ROI. However, the data showed that if they had conducted the coaching, it would have made a difference, which would be very positive.

When Kaycee presented this data to the executives, they also suspected that the coaching was not taking place. Even the managers responsible for coaching realized they were not stepping up to their challenge and carrying it out. Ultimately, this turned out to be a good experience for everyone because the managers changed their actions and began coaching more effectively. With the changes, the ROI became positive. Most importantly, the executives and managers said, "We love this kind of data. Please do more of these evaluations." Kaycee's experience underscores that even a negative ROI is okay. It forces improvement to make things better.[4]

The Work I Do Is Necessary, So Why Should I Improve It?

Ben Wagner is one of several software design testers for a large automobile maker in Europe. Ben's job is to test changes in software under various conditions to make sure it's working correctly. Ben and the team have been doing this manually for years. However, he noticed that the work had become routine and monotonous for the team. It was no longer enjoyable for many of them. The team's turnover was quite high, and the number of tests conducted (the productivity) seemed to be less than desired.

To address the issue, Ben explored using automatic testing with an Agile software developer. By automating the testing, the team could save a tremendous amount of work. In fact, with 32 people involved in software testing, automating the process would eliminate the need for these individuals, and they could be reassigned to more productive, engaging, and challenging work. In fact, the organization needed these team members in other places. The key was that the software testing had to be effective, reliable, and not so expensive.

Ben tried the new approach on an experimental basis and, yes, found that it worked and saved the company money. The ROI was high. As a result, his team considered him a hero. He had solved a major problem, allowing the team to assign software specialists to other needed projects. Even if what you do is essential, there may be an opportunity to improve it and share value across the enterprise.

Making the Case for a System-Wide Implementation

Kitana Kanaan is a business change officer at Byblos Bank in Beirut, Lebanon. Kitana volunteered for a project to automate the automobile loan process in the bank's branches. In this type of project, Kitana would normally search for the appropriate software, evaluate specific references, and implement the system. Kitana realized that this approach was not acceptable to others, and that the evaluation needed to be more concrete and convincing. Kitana began using the Show the Value Process and its five levels to show the value of this project. She detailed the specific reaction that she wanted individuals to have as they changed the process.

Previously, the car loan process took much longer than necessary, resulting in excessive amounts of paper that became a storage problem for the branches. Kitana believed that the proper use of this new software would dramatically decrease loan-processing time, reduce paper, and free storage space for other uses. She realized that individuals must learn how to use this system properly and fully understand the reasons for the change (learning). She also had to ensure that the system was used properly, and that the changes with paper usage were occurring (application). Finally, she detailed the impact of this process, tracking the time savings, paper reduction, and space allocation (impact). In addition, she tracked customer satisfaction as well as job satisfaction of the staff involved (intangible benefits). She became keenly aware of the corporate social responsibility of the bank in its paper reduction efforts. Kitana isolated the effect of the new project on the impact measures, converted it to money, and calculated the ROI—all on a pilot basis in one branch.

Using these data made a very convincing case for system-wide implementation of this process.

Leveraging Your Results to Help Others

Haifa Al Lawati, director of the Evaluation Department for the Ministry of Education in the Sultanate of Oman, was asked to find a reliable method to show the value of various programs for teachers, school principals, and other leadership and administrative staff. After searching for the right process to tackle this issue, Haifa settled on the approach described in this book. She received training in the Show the Value Process and then arranged training for others. Along with a team of other individuals, she developed several evaluations of various programs measuring the impact and sometimes even the ROI.

With the help of her team, she published a book, *Studies on ROI of Professional Development Programs*. This book was used internally to show others the value of these different projects and to gain support for more evaluation. She and her team earned a reputation of having programs that deliver results along with a willingness to show the results in a very credible way.

Her work began to spread to other government agencies in Oman, and she and her team began conducting workshops to teach others this process. This work helped to improve the quality of training programs in the ministry in many aspects and at various stages. Overall, this has helped in receiving continued funding and support for all types of professional development programs in the ministry.

Change the value of what you deliver by changing your thinking. Rather than think of showing value as a burden, consider it an opportunity to spotlight what works and what doesn't, so that you can help your organization or community in ways beyond the implementation of just one project. Communicate your project's results with confidence, use the results to improve, and leverage results to drive lasting change and create greater value.

The final step in the process shows the value of communicating, optimizing, and leveraging the results of your project. Showing the value of what you do in a systematic, logical process can make an amazing difference, as illustrated through the many examples throughout this book. Even if results are disappointing, as with Kaycee Buckley, you can leverage the results to create a positive outcome. The ROI in the Show the Value Process is not in the results it will help you deliver. The ROI is in how you use and leverage the results to achieve the purpose you set out to achieve when you answered the first question—Why?

So, there you have it, a process that can add value to your work, your projects, and you. This approach can make a difference in your success and the success of others around you.

ACTION STEPS

After completing this chapter, take the following action steps:

1. **Communicate results.** Make sure you select the appropriate audiences. Be as specific as possible.
2. **Optimize the results of this project.** Take action on the insights from the evaluation. Explain how you used the insights to improve the project and your work. Provide as much detail as possible.
3. **Leverage the results of this project.** Explain how you will use the results to improve the project, your organization, and your work.
4. **Read the next chapter.** The next chapter will provide tips to help you be successful with the Show the Value Process.

Making It Work

This book presents a step-by-step process you can use to show the success of any endeavor that may be part of your work or responsibility. It measures success along five levels: reaction, learning, application, impact, and ROI. By reading this book, you've learned how to do this; now you need to act. Just like any other activity, it's not what you know, but what you do. So, what do you do? Here are a few tips.

Clarify why you are evaluating this project. Begin with the end in mind. What do you wish to gain by doing this? When do you want to complete this evaluation? What will it look like? What types of data will you be presenting, and at what time?

Some of you have already begun using the chapters in the book to support your work. If you have not, begin now. The longer you wait, the more difficult it will be. We've never known anyone to start too early, but we've seen many start too late.

While this book provides a lot of information, other books provide even more. See the publication section of the website. The website (roiinstitute.net/show-the-value) offers tools and templates. If you need support, ask for help.

You may want to partner with a coach or mentor. This can be an informal or formal arrangement. The coach may be a friend, colleague, or a coach certified by ROI Institute. You might even consider participating in the group coaching available through the ROI Certification process. See the website for more details.

Remember that failure is okay. Progress is important. The cornerstone of this methodology is a relentless focus on process improvement. If it is successful, take action to make it even more successful next time. If your project is unsuccessful, take action to improve it. Addressing disappointing results is easier than we sometimes think.

Celebrate success. Apart from your sponsor, share your accomplishments with others. Other people need to know your outcomes. Let your community know. Let us publish your study! The key is to celebrate success and let others learn from it—better yet, let them replicate it.

If you need to learn more, a variety of formal learning programs are available. A one-day overview workshop provides the essentials. A more comprehensive train-the-trainer workshop is also available. Finally, for those who want to become a Certified ROI Professional (CRP), an intensive program is available that includes education, group coaching, and application. The program focuses on completing an ROI evaluation of a project to earn the CRP designation.

The important milestone is that you have learned a critical skill. Use this process routinely in your daily activities. The Show the Value Process keeps you focused and makes you aware of what's possible and what is required to make any effort successful. It will help you gain support and commitment from others. It will also help you gain funding in the future.

So, remember, when it comes to delivering results, hope is not a strategy, luck is not a factor, doing nothing is not an option. Change is inevitable; progress is optional. It's all up to you.

Show the Value of What You Do Discussion Guide

This discussion guide will help you facilitate small group discussions with those who are learning how to use the concepts in this book. The guide follows the chapters in the book.

INTRODUCTION: DELIVERING SUCCESS

1. Discuss the need to show the value of your specific projects, with specific examples.
2. What impact is this process having with you?
3. Specifically, who can benefit from using this process?
4. What is your current approach to delivering and measuring success? Are you stuck on the traditional approach?
5. How did you use the book's website material?

CHAPTER 1: SHOW THE VALUE PROCESS

1. How have you measured the success of a project? Be specific.
2. What is your reaction to the five levels of success? Are they logical and easy to understand?
3. What's your reaction to the six steps to deliver and measure success (Show the Value Process)? Contrast that with the five levels of success.

CHAPTER 2: WHY? START WITH IMPACT

1. How often do your projects begin with the end in mind and with a business measure?
2. What are the business measures for your project?
3. When does it become difficult to connect a project to a business measure?

4. Do you think there is a need for a project to deliver more value than it costs?

5. What is the danger of waiting for someone to ask you for impact and ROI?

CHAPTER 3: HOW? SELECT THE RIGHT SOLUTION

1. Is the solution usually obvious for a problem that you are tackling?
2. Is it always possible to find the right solution?
3. Describe a time when you had to identify the cause of a problem.
4. Why are learning and preference needs necessary?

CHAPTER 4: WHAT? EXPECT SUCCESS WITH OBJECTIVES

1. Is it appropriate to consider that the success of projects should be determined at the impact level? If so, why? If not, why not?
2. How often have you set very specific objectives for projects?
3. If objectives are so powerful, why don't we write and use them more often?
4. What are the objectives of your project?

CHAPTER 5: HOW MUCH? COLLECT DATA ALONG THE WAY

1. What data collection methods have you used?
2. What issues have you encountered in collecting data?
3. Do you think it is possible to collect the data you need for your project?
4. How can we improve the data collection process?
5. What methods of data collection will you use on your project?
6. How will you overcome the challenges of obtaining a good response rate?

CHAPTER 6: WHAT'S IT WORTH? ANALYZE THE DATA

1. Is it possible to isolate the effects of every project?
2. How will you isolate the effects of your project from other influences?

3. Is converting data to money a challenge for you?
4. Describe the power of intangibles and why they are important.
5. What costs will you include in your project?
6. Will you plan to calculate the ROI? If so, will you calculate both BRC and ROI?

CHAPTER 7: SO WHAT? LEVERAGE THE RESULTS

1. To whom will you communicate the results of your project?
2. What will be the purpose of this communication?
3. What method will you use to communicate the results?
4. What changes will you be making in your project to make it better?
5. What is your concern about having a negative ROI? How would you address this?
6. How will you leverage the results of your project?

Notes

CHAPTER 2

1. The Arbinger Institute, *The Outward Mindset: Seeing Beyond Ourselves* (Oakland, CA: Berrett-Koehler Publishers, 2016).

2. Avery Hartmans and Paige Leskin, "The History of How Uber Went from the Most Feared Startup in the World to Its Massive IPO," BusinessInsider.com, May 18, 2019, https://www.businessinsider.com/ubers-history

3. Patricia Pulliam Phillips, Jack J. Phillips, Gina Paone, and Cindi Huff-Gaudet, *Value for Money: How to Show the Value for Money for All Types of Projects and Programs in Governments, Non-Governmental Organizations, Nonprofits, and Businesses* (Hoboken, NJ: John Wiley & Sons, 2019), 111–113.

4. Jack J. Phillips and Patricia Pulliam Phillips, *Proving the Value of HR: How and Why to Increase ROI*, 2nd ed. (Alexandria, VA: SHRM, 2012), 247–282.

5. Phillips et al., *Value for Money*, 39–41.

CHAPTER 3

1. Ginger Luttrell and Michael Doane, *The Super User (R)evolution: Unleashing the Collaborative Forces Already in Your Enterprise* (Dallas, TX: Enterprise Alliance Press, 2017).

2. Linda Dahlstrom, "Beyond May 29: Lessons from Starbucks Anti-Bias Training—and What's Next," *Starbucks Newsroom*, July 2, 2018, https://stories.starbucks.com/stories/2018/beyond-may-29-lessons-from-starbucks-anti-bias-training-and-whats-next/

3. Frank Dobbin and Alexandra Kalev, "Why Doesn't Diversity Training Work?" *Anthropology Now* 10, no. 2 (September 2018).

4. William J. Rothwell, Carolyn K. Hohne, and Stephen B. King, *Human Performance Improvement: Building Practitioner Competence*, 3rd ed. (London: Routledge, 2018).

5. Jack J. Phillips, Frank Fu, Patricia Pulliam Phillips, and Hong Yi, *ROI in Marketing: The Design Thinking Approach to Measure, Prove, and Improve the Value of Marketing* (New York: McGraw-Hill, 2020).

6. William Malsam, "5 Notorious Failed Projects & What We Can Learn from Them," October 23, 2018, https://www.projectman ager.com/blog/failed-projects

CHAPTER 4

1. Martin Burt, *Who Owns Poverty?* (Wareham, Dorset, UK: Red Press, 2019).

2. J. Doerr, *Measure What Matters: How Google, Bono, and the Gates Foundation Rock the World with OKRs* (New York: Penguin, 2018).

CHAPTER 5

1. Priceonomics Data Studio, "Companies Collect a Lot of Data, but How Much Do They Actually Use?," Priceonomics, https:// priceonomics.com/companies-collect-a-lot-of-data-but-how-much-do/

2. Patricia P. Phillips, Jack J. Phillips, and Bruce Aaron, *Survey Basics* (Alexandria, VA: ASTD Press, 2013).

CHAPTER 6

1. Charles (Chip) Huth and Jack J. Phillips, "Measuring ROI in Leadership Development." A complete copy of this case study is available at ROI Institute, or access at https://www.roiinstituteacademy .com/products/free-tools/categories/1247772/posts/2149800738

2. Suzanne Schell, "Enhanced Recovery after Colorectal Surgery Impact and ROI Study." For more information on this case study, contact info@roiinstitute.net.

3. James Surowicki, *The Wisdom of Crowds: Why the Many Are Smarter Than the Few and How Collective Wisdom Shapes Business, Economics, Societies and Nations* (New York: Doubleday, 2004).

4. Patricia Pulliam Phillips, Jack J. Phillips, Gina Paone, and Cindi Huff-Gaudet, *Value for Money: How to Show the Value for Money for All Types of Projects and Programs in Governments, Non-Governmental Organizations, Nonprofits, and Businesses* (Hoboken, NJ: John Wiley & Sons Publishing, 2019), 261–263.

5. Paul Heaton, "Hidden in Plain Sight: What Cost-of-Crime Research Can Tell Us about Investing in Police," *Rand Corporation*, https://www.rand.org/pubs/occasional_papers/OP279.html

6. Gallup. The Relationship Between Engagement at Work and Organizational Outcomes: 2020 Q12 Meta-Analysis, 10th Edition. (October 2020), https://www.gallup.com/workplace/321725/gallup-q12 -meta-analysis-report.aspx?thank-you-report-form=1; and Seppälä, Piia & Mauno, Saija & Feldt, Taru & Hakanen, Jari & Kinnunen, Ulla & Tolvanen, Asko & Schaufeli, Wilmar. (2008). The Construct Validity of the Utrecht Work Engagement Scale: Multisample and Longitudinal Evidence. *Journal of Happiness Studies* 10: 459–481. doi:10.1007/s10902-008-9100-y.

7. Patricia Pulliam Phillips, Jack J. Phillips, and Rebecca Ray, *Measuring the Success of Employee Engagement: A Step-by-Step Guide for Measuring Impact and Calculating ROI* (Alexandria, VA: ATD Press, 2016).

8. Patricia Pulliam Phillips and Jack J. Phillips, "Measuring ROI in a Master's Degree Program," in *Value for Money: Measuring the Return on Non-Capital Investments, ROI Case Studies*, vol. 1 (Birmingham, AL: Business Writers Exchange Press, 2018), 149–172.

CHAPTER 7

1. Jessica Kriegel, *Unfairly Labeled: How Your Workplace Can Benefit from Ditching Generational Stereotypes* (Hoboken, NJ: Wiley, 2016), 145–492.

2. Patricia Pulliam Phillips, Jack J. Phillips, Gina Paone, and Cindy Huff-Gaudet, *Value for Money: How to Show the Value for Money for All Types of Projects and Programs in Governments, Non-Governmental Organizations, Nonprofits, and Businesses* (Hoboken, NJ: John Wiley & Sons, 2019), 345–352.

3. Suzanne Schell, "Enhanced Recovery After Colorectal Surgery Impact and ROI Study." For more information on this case study, contact ROI Institute.

4. Patricia Pulliam Phillips, Jack J. Phillips, and Rebecca Ray, *Proving the Value of Soft Skills: Measuring Impact and Calculating ROI* (Alexandria, VA: ATD Press, 2020).

Acknowledgments

Many people have shaped the process presented in this book. First, many thanks go to all the users of the Show the Value Process. To date, more than 8,000 organizations are using this process with approximately 20,000 individuals applying it to projects. We thank them not only for using this process but also for helping us shape it over the years.

Additionally, we thank those who have allowed us to tell their stories in this book. Your stories bring the process to life, and your experiences inspire others to pursue the journey to show value.

To our team members at ROI Institute: You represent the best team we've ever seen. Many of you picked up the slack while we took on this book, and we appreciate your efforts. Special recognition goes to our director of publications, Hope Nicholas, one of the best editors we've ever known. Usually, you think of hope as not being a strategy, but in the case of the publications from ROI Institute, Hope *is* our strategy. She does her job well. Thank you, Hope, for all your great efforts to bring this book from an idea to reality and to make sure the world knows about it.

We thank Berrett-Koehler for taking on this publication, particularly Steve Piersanti, the founder and former CEO of Berrett-Koehler. He is genuinely the best editor we've ever met, and we have met many. We had the pleasure of working with Steve even before the Berrett-Koehler days. He has made amazing contributions to this book, helping us shape it to the right audience and present it in the right way. Steve's work is magic.

From Patti: It was May 20, 1997, at Chappy's deli, when Jack and I first met. There, a planned one-hour meeting stretched to four hours. It was during that conversation, Jack offered me an opportunity to join him in his quest to help individuals, worldwide, create and show value through their work. Jack's constant effort to drive ROI is why the concept has reached ubiquity in disciplines that disregarded it in the past; why practitioners and their functions are lauded for their efforts to demonstrate ROI; and why measurement, evaluation, and ROI are the norms, not novelties. Jack is my inspiration, my husband, and above all else, my friend. Because he laid the groundwork, I have a platform on which I stand and share with others how they can show the value of their work. All I can say is, *thank you, Jack, for all that you have done, all that you do, and for our amazing journey. I love you.*

From Jack: For every book that we write together, one of us takes the lead. In this case, Patti took the lead because she is the best for this task. She is an engaging, skillful writer, and more importantly, she knows this process in and out. Patti is our best facilitator, a sought-after keynote speaker, an effective and articulate consultant, an outstanding coach (recognized as one of the 50 best in the world by the Thinkers50 organization), and a tenacious researcher. Patti brings a wealth of experience, but more importantly, she presents it in an engaging, interesting, and meaningful way. Above all, Patti is my best friend and a very loving spouse. She makes a difference in everything we do. *I love you for all you are and all you do.*

Index

Page numbers followed by letter f indicate a figure.

About the Authors

PATTI P. PHILLIPS, PH.D.

Patti P. Phillips, Ph.D., is the CEO of ROI Institute, Inc., the leading source of ROI competency building, implementation support, networking, and research. As author, researcher, consultant, and coach, Patti helps organizations implement the ROI Methodology® in more than 70 countries. Since 1997, Patti has led the adoption of the ROI Methodology and measurement and evaluation to drive organizational change. Her work spans private, public, nonprofit, and nongovernmental organizations.

Patti serves as a member of the board of trustees of the United Nations Institute for Training and Research (UNITAR). She is chair of the Institute for Corporate Productivity (i4cp) People Analytics Board; senior advisor, human capital, for The Conference Board; and board member of the International Federation for Training and Development Organizations (IFTDO). Additionally, she serves as board chair for the Center for Talent Reporting (CTR) and is a fellow of the Association for Talent Development (ATD) Certification Institute. Patti is also on the UN System Staff College faculty in Turin, Italy. Her work has been reported on CNBC and Euronews and published in more than a dozen business journals.

Patti's academic accomplishments include a bachelor's degree in education from Auburn University; a master's degree in public and private management from Birmingham-Southern College, and a Ph.D. in international development from the University of Southern Mississippi.

Patti, along with her husband, Dr. Jack J. Phillips, contributes to various journals and has authored books about measurement, evaluation, analytics, and ROI. In 2019, she and Jack received the Distinguished Contributor Award from the Center for Talent Reporting for their contribution to the measurement and management of human capital. In November 2019, Patti and Jack were named 2 of the top 50 coaches globally by the Thinkers50 organization, and they were finalists for the Marshall Goldsmith Distinguished Achievement Award for Coaching. Additionally, in May 2022, Patti and Jack received the Association for Talent Development's highest honor, the Thought Leader Award. Recipients of this award have contributed significant thought leadership to the talent development profession, which has had sustained impact over several years.

You can reach Patti at patti@roiinstitute.net.

JACK J. PHILLIPS, PH.D.

Jack J. Phillips, Ph.D., chair of the ROI Institute, is a world-renowned expert on accountability, measurement, and evaluation. Jack provides consulting services for Fortune 500 companies and major global organizations. The author or editor of more than 100 books, he conducts workshops and presents at conferences throughout the world.

Jack has received several awards for his books and work in addition to those received jointly with Patti. The Society for Human Resource Management presented him an award for one of his books and honored a Phillips ROI study with its highest award for creativity. In 2005, the Association for Talent Development awarded him its highest award, Distinguished Contribution to Workplace Learning and Development for his work on ROI. For three years, Meeting News recognized Jack as one of the 25 most influential leaders in the meetings and events industry based on his work on ROI. Jack's work has been featured in the *Wall Street Journal*, *BusinessWeek*, and *Fortune* magazine. He has been interviewed by several television programs, including CNN.

Jack's expertise in measurement and evaluation is based on more than 27 years of corporate experience in the aerospace, textile, metals, construction materials, and banking industries. Jack has served as training and development manager at two Fortune 500 firms, as senior human resource officer at two firms, as president of a regional bank, and as management professor at a major state university.

Jack regularly consults with clients in manufacturing, service, and government organizations in over 70 countries in North and South America, Europe, the Middle East, Africa, Australia, and Asia.

Jack has undergraduate degrees in electrical engineering, physics, and mathematics; a master's degree in Decision Sciences from Georgia State University; and a Ph.D. in Human Resource Management from the University of Alabama. He has served on the boards of several private businesses—including two NASDAQ companies—and several nonprofits and associations, including the American Society for Training and Development, the National Management Association, and the International Society for Performance Improvement, where he served as president (2012–2013).

Jack Phillips can be reached at jack@roiinstitute.net.

Berrett–Koehler
Publishers

Berrett-Koehler is an independent publisher dedicated to an ambitious mission: *Connecting people and ideas to create a world that works for all.*

Our publications span many formats, including print, digital, audio, and video. We also offer online resources, training, and gatherings. And we will continue expanding our products and services to advance our mission.

We believe that the solutions to the world's problems will come from all of us, working at all levels: in our society, in our organizations, and in our own lives. Our publications and resources offer pathways to creating a more just, equitable, and sustainable society. They help people make their organizations more humane, democratic, diverse, and effective (and we don't think there's any contradiction there). And they guide people in creating positive change in their own lives and aligning their personal practices with their aspirations for a better world.

And we strive to practice what we preach through what we call "The BK Way." At the core of this approach is *stewardship,* a deep sense of responsibility to administer the company for the benefit of all of our stakeholder groups, including authors, customers, employees, investors, service providers, sales partners, and the communities and environment around us. Everything we do is built around stewardship and our other core values of *quality, partnership, inclusion,* and *sustainability.*

This is why Berrett-Koehler is the first book publishing company to be both a B Corporation (a rigorous certification) and a benefit corporation (a for-profit legal status), which together require us to adhere to the highest standards for corporate, social, and environmental performance. And it is why we have instituted many pioneering practices (which you can learn about at www.bkconnection.com), including the Berrett-Koehler Constitution, the Bill of Rights and Responsibilities for BK Authors, and our unique Author Days.

We are grateful to our readers, authors, and other friends who are supporting our mission. We ask you to share with us examples of how BK publications and resources are making a difference in your lives, organizations, and communities at www.bkconnection.com/impact.

Dear reader,

Thank you for picking up this book and welcome to the worldwide BK community! You're joining a special group of people who have come together to create positive change in their lives, organizations, and communities.

What's BK all about?

Our mission is to connect people and ideas to create a world that works for all.

Why? Our communities, organizations, and lives get bogged down by old paradigms of self-interest, exclusion, hierarchy, and privilege. But we believe that can change. That's why we seek the leading experts on these challenges—and share their actionable ideas with you.

A welcome gift

To help you get started, we'd like to offer you a **free copy** of one of our bestselling ebooks:

www.bkconnection.com/welcome

When you claim your **free ebook**, you'll also be subscribed to our blog.

Our freshest insights

Access the best new tools and ideas for leaders at all levels on our blog at ideas.bkconnection.com.

Sincerely,

Your friends at Berrett-Koehler